Draw and Sketch
Landscapes
16 Projects in 6 steps or less

Janet Whittle

SEARCH PRESS

A QUARTO BOOK

Published in 2002 by Search Press Ltd.
Wellwood
North Farm Road
Tunbridge Wells
Kent
TN2 3DR

ISBN 1-903975-15-8

QUAR.LDL

Conceived, designed, and produced by
Quarto Publishing plc
The Old Brewery
6 Blundell Street
London N7 9BH

Senior Project Editor: Nicolette Linton
Senior Art Editor: Penny Cobb
Designer: Brian Flynn
Photographers: Colin Bowling,
                Paul Forrester
Copy editor: Hazel Harrison
Proofreader: Kate Phelps
Indexer: Pamela Ellis

Art director: Moira Clinch
Publisher: Piers Spence

Manufactured by
Universal Graphics Pte Ltd., Singapore
Printed by
Star Standard Industries Pte Ltd.,
Singapore

Contents

Introduction

For me, the joy of sketching is in its simplicity. You can take the minimum of equipment and go wherever the fancy takes you, stop and – in a minute or so – be busy working away on your chosen subject. No fuss, no frills and very rewarding. Whether or not you show the finished result to anyone does not matter; sketching makes you observe what otherwise might pass you by.

The time you spend sketching is up to you; you could take an hour or five minutes. I love to sketch one view, turn around and sketch another, and so on, experimenting with composition and light direction, then following the best as a blueprint for a painting. However, I enjoy sketching as an art form in its own right, often working on a quick sketch after returning home, while the scene is still in my imagination. Although photographs are an important reference tool, they do not capture the scents and sounds that trigger my imagination, so I make notes as well.

I try never to be without a sketchbook and camera. I learn something every time I go out, in different seasons and weathers and at different times of the day. Even if I stay close to home, I will always find a new angle on a view; the sky alone changes so rapidly.

One of the comments I hear most often is, 'sketching has opened up a whole new world to me. I never realised that I didn't look properly before'. You can miss so much and not know it, so get on out there!

Janet Whittle

Janet Whittle

Materials for projects

Below is a list of the materials you will need for each project. Use good-quality drawing paper unless otherwise stated.

Note that coloured pencils and pastels, in particular, are available in a vast range of colours and the names vary considerably from one manufacturer to another. For this reason, pastels and pencils are listed as generic colours (blue, green, for example) rather than as specific manufacturer's shades. Choose the colours from your preferred range that match the ones in the projects most closely.

The size of the brush you use will depend on your own personal taste and on the scale of the drawing you're producing. Brush sizes are therefore given as 'small' or 'medium', to give you a general guideline about what to select.

But don't worry if you don't have exactly the right equipment to hand: these projects are merely a stepping stone to help you develop your own ways of interpreting landscapes and, as always in art, keen observation is the key to success.

COUNTRY LANE • HB pencil • Range of soft graphite pencils from 3B to 9B

MOUNTAIN VIEW • HB pencil • 3B pencil • 9B pencil

SHALLOW RIVER • HB pencil • 2B pencil • 3B pencil • 9B pencil

FARM ROAD • HB pencil (optional) • Fountain pen • Black Chinese (or other water-soluble) ink • Watercolor paints: Payne's grey or indigo • Small round brush • Rigger brush • Medium to large round brush

ARIZONA LANDSCAPE • Brown conté stick • Putty eraser

PUMPKIN FIELD • Coloured pencils: green-grey, dull red, light orange, light blue, viridian or blue-green, light green, yellowish pale green, mid green, gold-orange, brick red, blue, grey, ochre, brown, red-violet, blue-violet

POPPY FIELD • Pastel paper • Charcoal pencil • Oil pastels: cobalt blue, pale blue-green, indigo, pale yellow-green, red, red-orange, orange (light and mid-tones), yellow, olive green, pink (light and mid-tones)

RED CLIFFS • Watercolour paper • 6B pencil • Watercolour paints: cadmium yellow, yellow ochre, cerulean blue, cobalt blue, light red, sap green, French ultramarine, viridian • Small round brush

SNOWY LANE • Watercolour paper • Carbon pencil • Watercolour paints: Cobalt Blue, Indigo, Burnt Sienna, Raw Sienna, Payne's Gray, Burnt Umber, Ultramarine Blue, Alizarin Crimson • Small round brush

WATERFALL • HB pencil • 3B pencil • 9B pencil

POND AND HAWTHORN BUSH • Ochre-coloured pastel paper • Pastel pencils: ochre, pale blue, purplish blue, greenish blue, dark green, mid green, blue green (light and mid-tones), yellowish green, creamy yellow, pink (pale and mid-tones), dark brown, yellow (mid- and deep tones)

PALM TREES • Sanguine conté crayon • Putty eraser • Spray fixative

TREES IN A CORNFIELD • HB pencil • 3B pencil • 9B pencil

TREES AND GATE • 3B or 4B pencil • Coloured pencils: lemon yellow, crimson, cobalt blue, burnt sienna, black, emerald green, indigo

SUNSET OVER WATER • Watercolour paper • 2B pencil • Pastels; olive green (mid- and dark tones), red, orange, lemon yellow, yellow (light and mid-tones), indigo

REFLECTIONS IN STILL WATER • Watercolour paper • HB pencil • Watercolour paints: cobalt blue, cadmium yellow, viridian, burnt umber, indigo, rose madder • Masking fluid • Riggerer brush • Small to medium round brush • Knife

Getting started

You don't need an extensive array of materials to begin sketching. It is better to start with as few as possible so that you don't misplace them or waste time deciding which to use. Your basic kit need consist of no more than a few pencils of various grades, an eraser and a sketchbook – or a drawing board and paper if you like to work on a large scale. As you progress, you may want to add a light folding chair and an easel to your kit, and a hat if you intend to work in bright sunlight. For outdoors, take a plastic bag to protect your work from the rain.

Sketching tips

Another useful sketching aid is a viewfinder, which is very helpful in deciding the viewpoint and composition. You can make one by cutting a rectangular hole in a piece of card or using two L-shaped pieces that can overlap one another to form a rectangle. When you look at a large expanse of landscape it can be hard to decide how much to include, but the viewfinder acts as a frame, isolating parts of the landscape.

If possible, include a camera in your kit so that you can take a reference photo in case you are unable to finish the sketch. And to avoid forgetting anything, make a checklist before you start. It is extremely frustrating to arrive at your destination and find you have forgotten the pencils or the eraser.

Basic kit *Three grades of pencil, an eraser and paper clipped onto a drawing board are all you need to get started.*

Camera and viewfinder *Take some photographs of the view to use as a reference aid when you get home. A viewfinder will help you decide on the composition.*

Starting to sketch

At first you will look for the perfect scene, and will probably waste a good deal of time going from one place to another, believing that the perfect place is just around the next corner, until you can become so confused you can't settle. The perfect scene very seldom exists; the key to a good sketch is the combination of the artist's imagination and the seen landscape features. You can alter

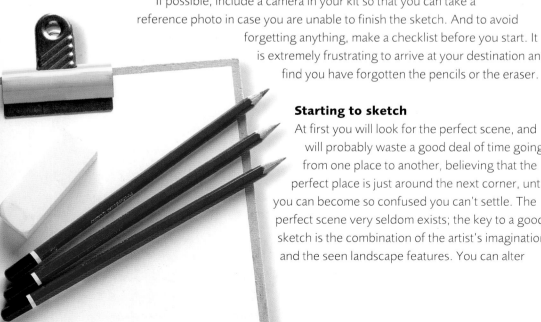

things in various ways to make a good drawing. For example, you might increase the tonal contrasts or change the light source. Most important of all, remember that you can leave things out. You don't want to include detail that clutters the picture, so decide what to focus on – one or two main features will usually be sufficient for a composition.

Once you are comfortable and have all your materials to hand, draw a border on your sheet before sketching in the main shapes. This is easier than using the edges of the paper as the 'frame' and also gives you the opportunity to expand the drawing if you need to. If you cannot decide on the composition, even with the viewfinder, make several small line drawings, trying different arrangements. This tends to focus the mind and get your imagination going, and the end result is often better than if you charge straight in. But above all, don't worry if your first attempts are disappointing; drawing requires practice, and you will succeed if you keep at it.

Checklist *To avoid frustration when sketching outdoors, make a list of the materials and equipment you need to take with you.*

CHECKLIST
✓ sketchbook
✓ Viewfinder
✓ Camera
✓ HB pencil
✓ 2B pencil
✓ 4B pencil
✓ Eraser
✓ Watercolour paints
✓ Paintbrushes
✓ Water jar

Plotting initial marks *Draw a border on your sheet before sketching in the main shapes.*

The Fundamentals

This section of the book outlines the basic principles and techniques that are fundamental to drawing and sketching. The section is divided into subject areas such as Using Colour or Perspective, and the information is conveyed through simple step-by-step exercises.

THE FUNDAMENTALS

Simple shapes

Most successful paintings and drawings are based on simple shapes such as squares, circles, ovals, oblongs and so on. You can't always identify these in a finished sketch, but they are there as underlying 'hidden' shapes, so try to look for these in the landscape before you start to draw.

Recognising simple shapes
Practise looking for the hidden simple shapes in a scene. Place an overlay over a photo and draw the main shapes with a soft pencil.

Using grids *You may find it helpful to use a squaring-up method to create your drawing. Create a grid as described (right). Decide on the size of your drawing, and draw the same number of squares on your paper. You can then transfer the information from your grid to your paper.*

Learning to simplify

The sheer variety of shapes in a landscape can be overwhelming when you first start to sketch, and you will be further confused by tones and colours, and by changing light, all of which can obscure the main shapes. The shape of a tree in full foliage is quite easy to see in a dull or low light, but much harder in bright sunlight, which creates a mass of small highlights and shadows. But with practice you will learn how to ignore the details, look for the main shapes and simplify them when you are composing the drawing or painting. Remember also to vary the sizes and the spacing of shapes such as trees, rocks or fields to give your work more interest.

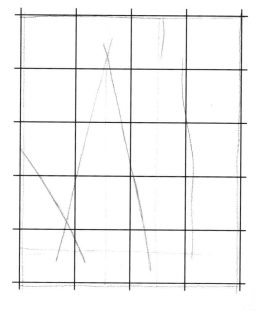

Making a grid
Fix a piece of stiff transparent material to the back of a piece of cardstock with the centre square cut out. Draw 1.5-cm (⁵/₈-inch) squares with a permanent felt-tip pen on the transparent material.

Thumbnail sketches

It may sound laborious to make small sketches before embarking on the main sketch, but it is helpful, as it can save you having to make changes later. The more preparation you do, the more chance you have of achieving a successful painting. Sketch in the main shapes and tonal values, restricting the tones to no more than five – or as few as three if possible. These thumbnails will concentrate the mind and highlight possible mistakes that could result in your having to make major changes to correct the work.

When you begin on the drawing or painting, simplify brushstrokes and pencil lines so that the viewer is not confused as to what the picture is about, and leave detail until last when you can decide how much to include. Sometimes you will need very little, so don't try to draw in every cloud, every leaf or branch on a tree, or every ripple on water. These are usually just as effective, or even more so, if they are merely suggested rather than treated literally.

Thumbnail sketches *To avoid basic mistakes in the composition, do a quick sketch of the main shapes using between three and five tonal values.*

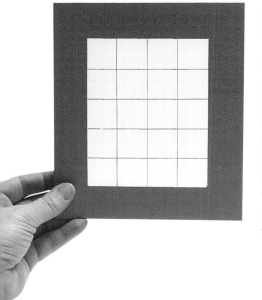

EXERCISE I

Country lane by Janet Whittle

When you are sketching outdoors directly from the subject, you will see a lot more than is reproduced in a photo, so you may have to be selective. However, one of the advantages is that you can move around and explore different viewpoints and compositional possibilities. To make a better composition, the artist has widened the path leading into the composition and slightly altered the smaller tree on the left.

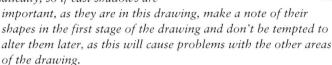

Remember that on a sunny day the pattern of light and shade will alter dramatically, so if cast shadows are important, as they are in this drawing, make a note of their shapes in the first stage of the drawing and don't be tempted to alter them later, as this will cause problems with the other areas of the drawing.

Practice points

- MAKING A NOTE OF SHADOW PATTERNS
- LOOKING FOR NEGATIVE SHAPES
- COMPOSING THE DRAWING

STAGE 1
MAKE AN OUTLINE DRAWING

■ Mark in the boundaries of the drawing, which will help you to place the main features, and then make a simple outline drawing with an HB pencil. Keep the lines fairly light, as most of these will not be wanted in the finished drawing and they will be erased later.

To help you draw the tree correctly, look for the 'negative' shapes where the sky shows between the branches. These shapes are simpler than the 'positive' ones of the trunk and branches, and are a useful double-check when drawing.

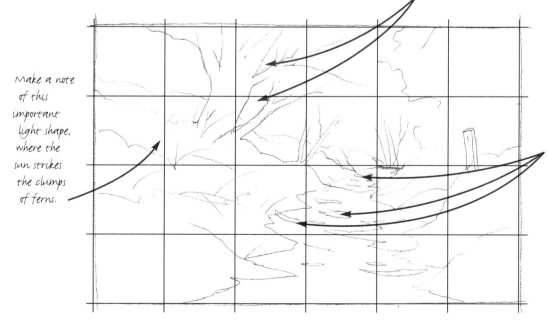

Make a note of this important light shape, where the sun strikes the clumps of ferns.

Draw the shapes of the little patches of light carefully, as they will change as the sun moves. Make them smaller towards the end of the lane to create the sense of recession.

STAGE 2
START THE SHADING

■ Begin at the top of the drawing to avoid smudging and work from left to right – or the reverse if you are left-handed. Use an HB pencil at this stage to produce tones in the light to middle range.

Make diagonal strokes to suggest grasses or non-specific foliage, varying the angles and finishing with dots and tiny squiggles at the top.

Now that some tone has been filled in behind the trunk, the tree itself becomes a simple light-against-dark shape, which makes it easier to 'read'.

Vary the strokes to suggest the different types of foliage, making small broken marks for the distant tree.

Draw the outlines of the leaves on the right-hand tree, as this is to be left mainly light against dark.

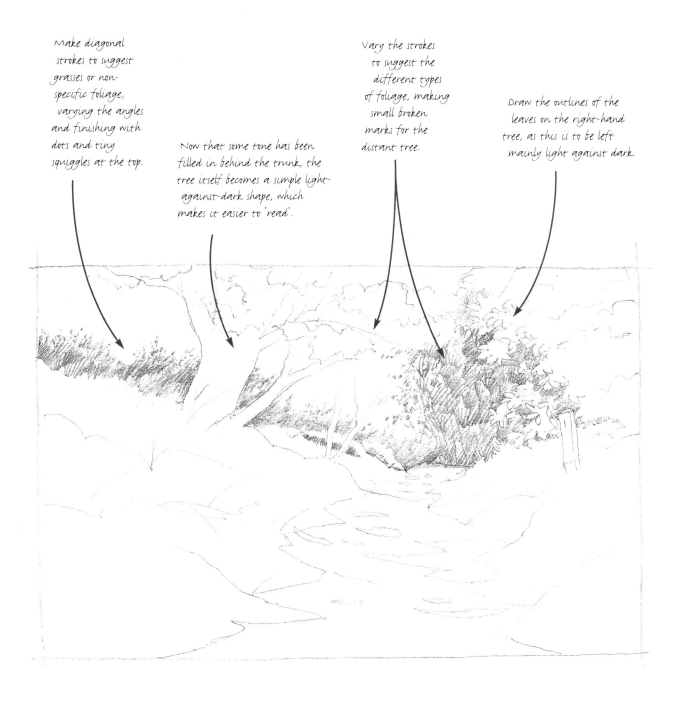

STAGE 3
BRING IN THE DARKS

■ Now you can begin to build up some dark tones in the background. Once these are established it will be easier to decide how to balance them with shadows and other dark areas in the foreground.

Using a 3B pencil, shade the large tree, leaving the foliage clumps white, then erase the lines of the tree where they go through the clumps.

Again with the 3B, draw the small trunks at the far end of the lane and deepen the tone slightly behind them so that they don't stand out too much.

Put in more shading in the negative space behind the larger leaves on the right.

STAGE 4
BUILD UP THE DRAWING

■ A first tone now needs to be laid on the lane and foreground foliage before more work is done on the trees. Take care to leave areas of the paper white to suggest the dappled sunlight effect.

Vary the pencils from 3B to 9B for the real darks, add more tone to the large tree trunk, then build up the foliage and shade in the small silver birch. Add more tone to some of the darker areas behind the post.

As you work towards the front of the drawing, lightly draw the main veins of the ferns as a guide, then shade around them to make them stand out.

Using an HB pencil, shade in the lane, with long strokes going slightly up at the edges to give the impression of the upward curve.

To suggest form and texture on the banks, use mainly short strokes, making longer, slightly curved strokes for the area beneath the main tree.

STAGE 5
BALANCE THE TONES

■ In the previous stage, the artist concentrated all of the dark tones at the back of the picture, keeping the foreground pale by comparison. The tonal pattern now needs to be built up, with the darks of the trees balanced by other dark areas in the foreground. Use a 3B pencil alone for this stage.

Deepen the tone behind some of the bracken on the left and take the same dark tone up the right bank.

To make a strong light/dark contrast in the immediate foreground, simplify the ferns in order to continue the tree shadows across the track.
This also helps to unite the foreground and middleground.

Darken the tones on the lane, working from top to bottom, and following your original lines for the shapes of the sunlight patches. If you find you have left too many, some can be toned down later.

STAGE 6
ADDITIONS AND MODIFICATIONS

■ Now that the drawing is almost complete, you should stand back from it (place it about 1 metre [3 feet] away) and decide whether adjustments are needed. You may find that more details or dark tones need to be added or that some of the light areas should be 'knocked back' by blending. You can also erase any guidelines that are still visible. You may wish to spray the completed drawing with pencil fixative, but this is optional.

J. WHITTLE

The artist has decided to bring in some puddles to add interest and to suggest sunlight after a squall of rain. Shade the small reflections with vertical strokes, using two tones for variety.

Deepen the tone of the trees at the end of the lane so that the shapes of the light leaves stand out well.

Darken and thicken the main shadow, shading over one or two of the light patches, and taking the shadow up the right bank to unite the left and right sides of the drawing.

Blend back some of the left-hand foreground areas with an HB pencil. Too many lights can create a confused, jumpy impression, but as in watercolour painting, it is better to have too many and blend back than not leave enough.

THE FUNDAMENTALS

Tonal values

The word tone, or value, simply describes the lightness or darkness of any colour, regardless of its hue. Tone is just as important in painting as it is in monochrome work, as both require a good balance of lights and dark and sufficient contrast to accentuate important features of the composition.

Restricting tonal values

You can see a great many values in nature, but if you try to include them all your work will become either confused or dull, possibly both, so try to identify the main values. Initially, you could start by dividing the composition into just three main values: light, medium and dark. Pay special attention to the focal point of the picture, as you want sufficient value contrast to emphasise it. A tree or house on the skyline painted in the same tone as the sky behind it will appear bland and flat, even if there is a contrast of colour.

From colour to tonal values *One easy way of finding out the tonal values in a photograph is to photocopy it in black and white.*

Identifying tonal values

Values are not always easy to identify, because the colour of an object is what we first see. It is helpful to squint your eyes, which cuts out much of the detail and reduces the impact of the colour; you will often see artists doing this when working on the spot. Making a tonal value chart, as shown below, is another way of avoiding mistakes and is especially useful in sketching with colour, where it is easy to get the values wrong. When you need to check whether a value is dark enough, hold up the strip and close one eye, select the value in the chart that is closest to the one required and place the equivalent colour on your painting. Often you will find you have not made it dark enough.

Tonal value chart *To make a tonal value chart, divide a sheet of watercolour paper into 10 even squares and number them one to 10. Leave the first square white. Using Payne's grey or burnt umber (as shown here), paint the second square in a very light tone and gradually darken the following squares until number 10 is as dark as possible (you may need two coats for this).*

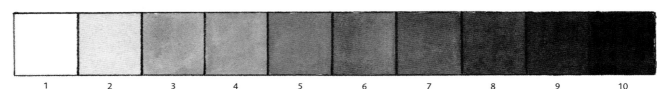

| 1 | 2 | 3 | 4 | 5 | 6 | 7 | 8 | 9 | 10 |

Colour values

Some colours are lighter in value than others. For example, yellow is always at the light end of the scale, and most blues and purples, if undiluted, are towards the dark end. These differences are known as tonal ranges; the darker you can make the colour (undiluted), the greater the value range. You need to understand this in order to darken colour mixtures, which you can do with those with a long tonal range, such as Payne's grey, burnt umber, and indigo, but not with the yellows and pinks, which have a short value range.

Changing shadows

If you are working on the spot, the shadows will change as the sun moves throughout the day. Sketch in these shapes at the start, and avoid trying to change the picture as you go on.

Checking value
Hold your tonal value chart up to the view and make sure you pick the right value. It is a common mistake to make the value too light.

9

5

3

2

Changing light
Note the effect of the light on the same scene sketched throughout the day. The long evening shadows in the third sketch add extra contrast and tonal value.

EXERCISE 2

Mountain view by Janet Whittle

This photograph of Yosemite National Park in California was taken on a slightly hazy day, which has simplified the details and reduced the tonal contrasts. To give the drawing more punch, the artist has strengthened the light to enable her to exploit the interplay of light and dark tones. This is easy enough to do; just decide where the light is coming from and make the shadows consistent. You will often have to do this when sketching outdoors, as weather can change rapidly, and even if it stays sunny, the sun moves constantly, completely changing the shadows and tonal patterns.

Practice points
- CONTROLLING TONES
- USING DIFFERENT GRADES OF PENCIL
- DRAWING TREES AND ROCKS
- INVENTING A LIGHT SOURCE

STAGE 1
THE DRAWING
■ Think about the composition before you start and decide whether you might leave a few things out. The fallen tree trunk in the water does not help the composition, and the foreground area would be strengthened by adding some dark reflections. Draw the main shapes lightly with an HB pencil.

Mark in the top line and the main vertical lines of the cliff.

This mass of foliage is quite confusing, as it is so near that you can see the individual leaves rather than the main shape. Exercise artistic licence to turn it into a simple shape.

Be precise with the angle of the tree, or you may have problems later on.

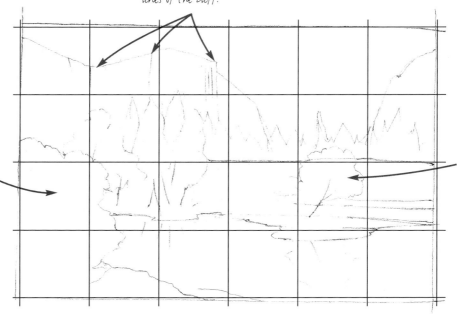

STAGE 2
START THE SHADING

■ Begin at the top of the picture, keeping the tones fairly light, but taking care to establish the really light areas by placing them next to a mid-tone. Notice how the cliff against the sky goes from dark against light at the top to light against dark on the right side. This is known as counterchange and is very important in tonal drawing.

shade the cliff, using vertical strokes that follow the direction of the rock formation.

Lightly draw in a few cloud shapes as a guide and shade above and between them, in the areas that would be blue, with an HB pencil.

Make this cliff a bit darker than the other so that the small patch of sky beside it shows up.

STAGE 3
ADD THE DARKS

■ Now you can start to put in some of the dark tones that will help you to build up the overall tonal pattern of the drawing.

Balance the darks of the trees with a dark shadow at the edge of the river bank, using the 3B pencil.

shade in the conifers with an HB pencil, changing to a 3B for the ones against the right-hand cliff. Don't make the tones so dark that you will be unable to add more on top for the shadowed area; even these dark trees are lighter on the side where the light strikes.

shade around the tree on the river bank, as areas of this will be left as white paper.

Draw in the trunks and lightly shade behind them, to give an idea of the way the trees grow.

STAGE 4
BUILD UP TONES

■ Begin the work on the trees in the middleground, using larger and more positive pencil marks, as these are nearer to you than the conifers, and you can see more foliage detail.

Darken the tones in a few places along the river bank using a 3B and then a 9B pencil.

Vary the marks so that they describe the different types of foliage and leave patches of white to suggest sunlight.

Put in a second tone on the conifers, leaving some of the trunks as mid-tone negative shapes.

STAGE 5
BRING IN THE DETAILS

■ You have now reached the most enjoyable part of any drawing, which is developing the foreground and starting to draw in details. It is always a temptation to add detail too early, but it is important to have the basic framework in place first.

Shade in the tree on the far left, behind the foreground bush.

Draw in one or two leaf shapes on the foreground tree and then shade the water behind, using first horizontal and then vertical strokes.

Draw in some stones beneath the water in the foreground and draw smaller stones on the bank beyond, darkening behind some of those nearest to the water.

Draw the reflections with the HB pencil, using vertical strokes and making the reflected tree trunks darker than the surrounding areas.

STAGE 6
COMPLETE THE DRAWING

■ Apart from a few final touches, all that now remains is to draw in the foreground tree. Like the cliff and sky, this tree and the one behind it are an example of counterchange, with the light edge of one set against the dark area of the other. The artist has deliberately exaggerated this effect; if you look back at the photo, you will see that the tree was quite formless, with little or no tonal contrast to separate it from the one behind it.

Using an HB pencil, shade in the foreground grass and tree, varying the pencil marks to suggest texture, leaving white paper at the edges of the tree.

Using a 3B and then a 9B pencil, deepen the tones of the foliage in places so that there are fewer patches of white paper.

Darken the reflections and the cracks between the underwater stones, then break up the reflections by making horizontal strokes with the edge of an eraser. Finally, draw in a few ripples leading into the central white band.

Shallow river by Janet Whittle

The shallowness of the water allows you to see the stones on the stream bed in the foreground, which make an interesting feature to sketch.

Practice points

· **SIMPLIFYING SHAPES AND DETAILS**

· **RESTRICTING THE TONAL RANGE**

· **VARYING THE PENCIL MARKS**

The bright sunlight provides a strong tonal pattern, with the pale shapes of the stones and the light bouncing off the water in the foreground contrasting with the darker areas of water. The strongly lit tree on the bank, which is the focal point of the composition, is set against the dark trees behind, producing what is known as counterchange (the lightest tone against the darkest). Counterchange is very important in monochrome drawing, as it adds depth as well as creating an impact.

STAGE 1

THE FRAMEWORK

■ Using an HB pencil, start with an outline drawing, looking for the main shapes and trying to simplify the rocks slightly to avoid a cluttered look. You can add more detail later if needed, but if you put in too much at the beginning you will become confused.

Draw these areas of light and dark tone as simple shapes at this stage.

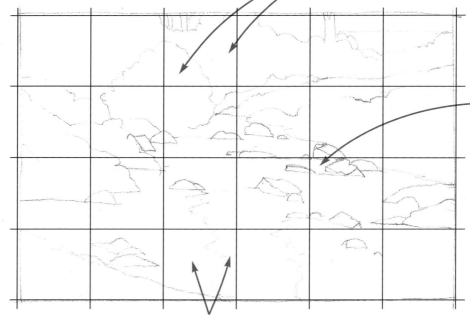

Look for the angle at which the rocks are set, bearing in mind that water has a horizontal plane.

sketch in the light area where the sun strikes, but don't work on the stones on the river at this stage, as the foreground will be left until later.

Keep the pencil strokes fairly consistent in direction, but vary the tones a little by increasing the pressure in places.

STAGE 2
START THE SHADING

■ Begin at the back of the drawing, with the area of dark tone. This is a large area to shade, so try to be consistent with your strokes so that it does not appear muddled; this could lead to complications later on.

This shadow at the top of the grassy bank will be a lighter tone than the background trees, so take care not to obscure the original drawn line.

Leave these areas as white paper, taking the pencil shading carefully around the edges.

STAGE 3
BUILD UP THE DARKS

■ Where there is a strong, dominant area of dark tone it is wise to establish this at an early stage, as it will provide a key for judging the strength of tone needed for the smaller dark areas in the middleground and foreground.

Change to a 3B pencil and put in the second tone on the background bushes to build up the counterchange.

Use more varied marks to suggest the forms and textures of the foliage, and leave patches of the original mid-tone showing.

Still using the HB pencil, shade in the tussocks of grass on the left bank.

The dark tone above defines the mid-tone area where the bushes are casting a shadow.

STAGE 4
INTRODUCE TEXTURE

■ Texture is an important theme in the drawing, with the smoothness of the rocks and water surface contrasting with the roughness of the trees. As you build up the drawing, think about how you can use the pencil marks to suggest the textures without becoming too fussy.

Using an HB pencil, texture the main tree, varying the marks from long hatching strokes to short squiggles. Leave white paper on the left side and top, where the sun strikes.

To push the light tree forwards, darken some areas behind it with a 3B and a 9B pencil.

Shade in the right bank, using marks that follow the directions of the clumps of grass. Make the marks shorter in the distance to suggest recession.

Draw in the bottoms and shaded sides of the rocks with an HB pencil.

Loosely draw in the foreground grasses, using a double line for each blade.

STAGE 5
DRAW THE ROCKS AND WATER

■ Now that you have established the main framework of tones, you can think about how the rocks, water and shadowed areas of the banks are to be treated. Try to restrict yourself to three tones rather than trying to reproduce every tone you can see in the subject, as this would weaken the impact of the drawing.

Deepen the second tone on the right and left banks to throw the light surfaces of the rocks into relief.

Put the first tone on the water, making horizontal strokes with an HB pencil and shading behind the foreground grasses. Make the strokes shorter in places to suggest the way the rocks break the surface.

Draw in some of the underwater rocks and stones in the shaded areas, varying the shapes and fading towards the light areas.

Begin to work the dark and mid-tones on the rocks and water, noting that the light is coming from the left, so the shadows will be on the right.

STAGE 6
FINAL ADJUSTMENTS

■ The tones now need to be strengthened here and there to balance the drawing, and the water needs some further definition to emphasise the play of light. Take care not to overwork in these final stages and to lay a clean piece of paper over the drawing to avoid smudging completed areas.

Use an HB pencil to blend and soften the background bushes so the focus is more on the river.

Deepen parts of the left and right banks, especially behind the rocks; then shade over some of the light tones to simplify them and make the composition easier to read.

Use an eraser to lift out a sweep of light tone across the water, then draw in one or two foreground ripples with a 3B pencil.

Deepen the dark cracks between the underwater stones, varying the lines from light to dark and from thick to thin, and making them lighter as they go back into the drawing. Using a 2B pencil, blend all the stones back with horizontal strokes.

THE FUNDAMENTALS

Other monochrome media

Although graphite pencils are the most commonly used drawing implements, there are many other tools for monochrome drawing, all of which are worth experimenting with. Your choice will ultimately depend on your individual style and the scale of your work. The colour you choose does not necessarily have to be grey or sepia. A monochrome sketch works better in colours with a long tonal range.

Trees on a hill
Charcoal can produce a sensitive line as well as texture and tonal value.

Tonal drawing

If you want to build up tones quickly in a drawing, you have two basic options. You can either lay the areas of tone with a water-based medium and a brush, or choose a soft, easy-to-smudge medium such as charcoal or conté crayon. Neither of these is ideal for outdoor sketching unless you work on a large scale. Charcoal, for example, can smudge more than you want and make a mess of your hands. However, for studio work, both can produce exciting results, as they allow you to build up tones rapidly, and in the case of charcoal you can lift out highlights with a putty eraser to achieve dramatic contrasts of light and dark.

Both charcoal and conté crayon come in pencil versions, which are easier to control and can produce both tone and sharp line. Another type of pencil that is useful for tonal drawing is the water-soluble coloured pencil, which you can wash over with water to create tones. Although coloured pencils are often sold in sets, you can usually buy the black ones separately. Don't forget to take a brush and water with you if you are working outdoors.

Dry media
Choose from the wide range of graphite and coloured pencils available on the market. Or try conté crayons or charcoal for tonal drawings. Lift out highlights from a charcoal sketch with a putty eraser for a dramatic effect.

Water pot *This collapsible water pot is ideal for sketching outdoors.*

Wet media *You can create a variety of effects with a pen and ink or a felt-tip pen, especially if you lay a wash over a non-soluble line.*

'Drawing' with a brush and ink is an excellent way of recording impressions quickly. This was a method much used by Rembrandt for both small landscape sketches and figure work. You can either use inks, which you can water down to produce a variety of tones, or one colour of watercolour such as a grey or brown.

Tone and line

Wash drawings can be combined with pen (or with charcoal or conté pencil) in a well-known technique known as line and wash (see pages 30–33). The choice of pens is a personal one – there is a huge variety of different drawing pens on the market, and fortunately most art shops allow you to try them out to decide whether you like a thick or thin line, a felt-tip or ballpoint pen. When choosing pens, decide whether or not you want the lines to run when washes are laid over them, that is, whether to use non-soluble or water-soluble pens. The latter can produce very effective results, since parts of the line will be softened as washes are laid over them. Use this method carefully, as some lines can be lost if softened too much.

Reflections in water *Objects reflected in still water produce an exact mirror image. This can result in the loss of the horizontal surface of the water, especially when using a monochrome medium. Lift out horizontal sweeps of colour with a tissue.*

Use a paler tonal value in the distance.

The light is coming from the left.

Ensure that the reflections of the trees lie directly beneath the actual trees.

The water looks dark against the light grass in the foreground.

Farm road by Janet Whittle

In this pen-and-wash sketch, watercolour has been used for the tone and a fountain pen with black Chinese ink for the line.

Chinese ink is sold in a round solid tablet and is very easy to use, but if you can't obtain it, any water-soluble black ink will do.

If you are not confident about drawing directly with the pen, you can draw the outline with an HB pencil, which you can erase later if necessary.

Practice points
- COMBINING LINE AND TONE
- BALANCING LIGHTS AND DARKS
- PLANNING THE COMPOSITION
- WORKING WET-IN-WET

STAGE 1
START THE DRAWING

■ Work out the composition before you start to draw – you can make a couple of rough sketches if you are unsure of how to treat the subject. Here, the artist has cropped the path at the front of the composition to make more of the trees, fence and pile of logs, which she saw as the main points of interest.

Keep the outline drawing as simple as possible, especially if you are working directly in ink, which you can't erase.

Cropping the path has provided a strong near-diagonal that leads the eye into the picture.

Artistic licence has been exercised here to turn the rather untidy pile of wood into a series of more orderly but interesting shapes.

STAGE 2
ADD TONE

■ Mix up a dark and a mid-tone of either Payne's grey or indigo and start painting from the back, dampening the background first with clean water.

With the lighter mix and a round brush, wash in the small area of sky behind the distant houses. While still slightly damp, put in the trees with the darker mix. Working wet-in-wet requires some practice; if the trees disappear into the first wash, it means the paper was still too wet, so wait thirty seconds and then try again.

Allow the washes for the sky and trees to dry, then paint in a varied wash with the lighter tone, leaving the tree tops on the right white, and painting in-between the fencing.

Dampen the paper in this area and work wet-in-wet as for the sky and trees, dropping the dark tone into the lighter one.

STAGE 3
REINFORCE THE LINE DRAWING

■ There are different ways of approaching pen-and-wash drawings. Some artists will complete the line drawing before adding tone, and others will reverse the process, drawing over washes. Here the two are used together, with more line added before the next wash.

Draw in the branches and twigs, taking care not to make them all follow the same direction; some branches come towards you, while others bend away.

shade the tree trunks fairly heavily, suggesting the textures with varied lines, then darken the shadowed sides of the fence posts to give them form.

Using the lighter of the two watercolour tones, put in a few background bushes and lay the same tone over some of the branches.

Draw some foliage on the banks, and darken around the log ends and towards the grass on the log pile.

STAGE 4
BUILD UP THE TONES

■ A little more drawing will be done as the sketch nears completion, but this stage is worked in tone alone, so mix up more of the first two tones if needed and then mix a third, very pale tone.

Work the left bank wet-in-wet, using the mid- and dark tones, and while the paper is still damp, pull out a few grasses with a rigger brush.

Wash over the path with the pale tone, using a medium to large brush. While still damp, sketch in the tracklines with the mid-tone, changing to the dark one as the tracks come towards you and widening the lines. Leave to dry.

STAGE 5
FINALISE THE DRAWING

■ Now comes what must be the most enjoyable part of any drawing: adding detail, firming up the drawing and adjusting tones where needed. Don't overdo things or the drawing could become busy, but do consider how the composition might be strengthened. For example, the foreground shadow and touches of line drawing suggest pebbles, ruts and grasses; these provide a balance for the other areas of the picture.

Break up the smooth line between the bank and track with grass texture, and then lay a pale tone over part of the log pile. Define the tree in the middleground with squiggly marks to suggest the foliage texture.

sketch in a light wash on the fence, trees and some of the foliage in front of the fence, and then add more line drawing on the trunks and branches.

sketch the shadow with a mid- to dark tone, leaving small patches of the lighter tone showing to suggest sunlight; then darken the tracks within the shadow and add touches of detail with the pen.

Build up the textures of the left bank with more line drawing, using the pen fairly heavily; make sure you leave patches of white paper showing through on the right side.

EXERCISE 5

Arizona landscape

by Barry Freeman

This powerful subject, with its strong, dramatic shapes and contrasts of tone, is well suited to a monochrome treatment. However, the artist has decided to work with brown rather than black conté crayon because it gives a better 'feel' of the hot colours of the landscape. He has changed the composition slightly from that seen in the photograph, first by leaving out the small central bush and its shadow, and second by simplifying the foreground trees so that they make a horizontal line at the front of the picture plane. This makes the composition more powerful by dividing it into three distinct bands, with the rocks as the dominant feature.

Practice points

- **DRAWING WITH CONTE CRAYON**
- **SUGGESTING TEXTURES**
- **EDITING THE SUBJECT**
- **VARYING THE PRESSURE**

STAGE 1

PLAN THE DRAWING

■ Start by making an outline drawing of the main shapes, using a corner of the conté stick, which will make a sharp line. If you make a mistake, lift out the incorrect line with a putty eraser. When you are satisfied with the outlines, begin to indicate the paler tones on the rocks and foreground trees.

Using the conté stick on its side, shade in the pale and mid-tones, keeping the pressure light, especially on the left, where the planes of the rocks catch the sunlight.

Use slightly heavier pressure here, as these areas are in shadow.

For the foreground foliage, combine side strokes with sharp lines to give an indication of both forms and textures.

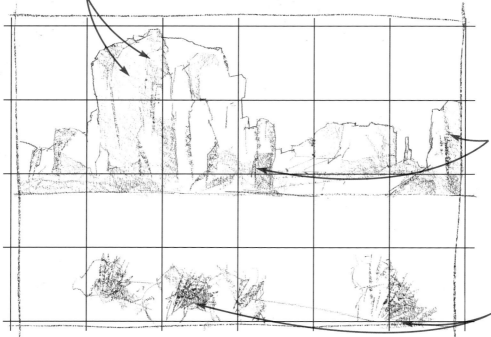

STAGE 2
BUILD UP THE TONES

■ In most monochrome drawings, the tones are built up gradually, working from light to dark, so at this stage you can start to indicate the stronger shadows. Pay special attention to the shapes of the shadows, as it is these that describe the structures.

To give form to the rocks, vary the shadows, from hard-edged ones to describe the flat planes to softer ones suggesting the more rounded forms.

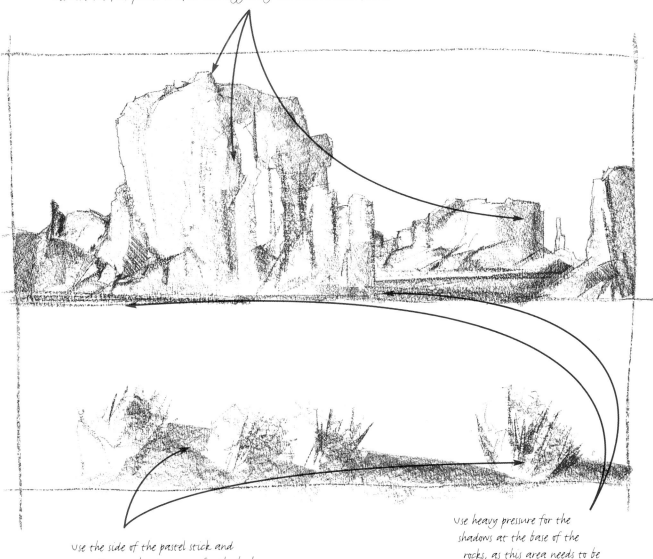

Use the side of the pastel stick and medium-to-hard pressure for the bushes and shadows. Then draw a few spiky lines with the corner of the stick.

Use heavy pressure for the shadows at the base of the rocks, as this area needs to be dark to separate it from the pale expanse of sand below.

STAGE 3
INCREASE THE PRESSURE

■ Continue to build up the strength of tone gradually, using the conté stick more heavily, but taking care to reserve the sunstruck areas as white or near-white paper.

Develop the structure and forms of the rocks with firm strokes. The central crevice and rectangular shadow on the right-hand rock play an important part in the composition, as they provide verticals to balance the horizontal band below.

The side of the rock structure is lightly covered with conté to suggest texture, but the tone is so pale that it would not stand out against the white sky, so the outline is important.

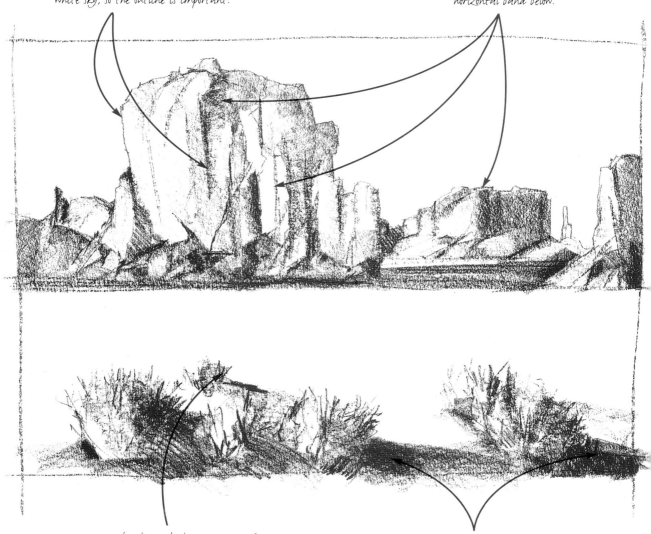

To break up the large expanse of sand and lead the eye in towards the rocks, draw in the small bush and its shadow.

Use very firm pressure for the shadow areas of the scrub. A dark tone is needed here to balance those on the rocks.

STAGE 4
TIE IT TOGETHER

■ The final stages are to darken the tones even more in places and to tie the two areas of the composition together by indicating the texture and pattern of the central area of sand.

Continue to heighten the contrast by building up the darkest shadows, using maximum pressure.

strengthen the tone of these two small shapes to make them stand out in relief against the white sky.

sketch in the sand ripples very loosely. They are important in making a link between the immediate foreground and the rocks, but treating them in too much detail would weaken the composition.

THE FUNDAMENTALS

Using colour

Pastels are a delightful medium for landscape sketches. It is easy to move on from drawing with a lead pencil or coloured pencils to using pastels as you are basically still using paint and drawing media. However, they are messy, and you will need to include some kind of hand-cleaning equipment in your kit, such as wet wipes or a paper towel.

Poppy field
The bright splash of red at the front of this work contrasts well with the gathering stormclouds.

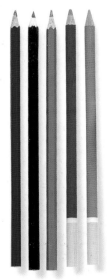

Dry media
Pastels and coloured pencils are ideal media for outdoor work, as they are easily portable.

Drawing with colour

Pastels are also obtainable in pencil form, which are less messy to use and perhaps more convenient for outdoor work. They are harder than most pastel sticks, allowing you to make more use of line, but areas of colour can be built up quickly. A related medium is coloured pencils, which are also popular for outdoor sketching. For anyone who likes strong, bold effects, felt-tip pens are worth trying. These are filled with coloured inks in a range of vivid, clear hues, and are either water-soluble or alcohol based. Coloured inks can also be bought for use with a brush, but although these look very enticing, they are inconvenient for outdoor work. The bottles are much heavier than tubes of paint, pens or pencils, and it is all too easy to spill ink or drop it on your clothes while taking brush to paper. However, they are worth trying for studio work, and have more potential than the ink pens, as colours can be mixed on a palette or watered down if required.

Watercolour and gouache

Watercolour has always been a favoured medium for working outdoors. It is easy to see why, as a good watercolour landscape has a freshness and immediacy that is hard to rival. It is also convenient, as the equipment is relatively portable, and you can record your impressions fairly quickly once you have learned how to mix and apply the colours. But there are other good mediums for landscape sketching, such as gouache. Gouache is

Colour wheel
Make a simple colour wheel showing the primary colours – red, blue, and yellow – and the secondary colours that derive from the primaries when mixed.

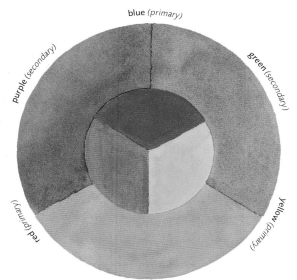

blue *(primary)*
purple *(secondary)*
green *(secondary)*
red *(primary)*
yellow *(primary)*
orange *(secondary)*

Wet media *Buy watercolour tubes and tablets individually as some colours, such as burnt umber, will be used up before others. Choose whether you want water-soluble or non-soluble felt-tip pens, depending on the effect you wish to achieve.*

the opaque version of watercolour and can be easier to use. The colours don't run into one another so freely, you can add light colors over dark ones, and mistakes can be corrected by overpainting with thicker colour.

Colour relationships

The colour wheel above also demonstrates the relationships between colours. Each primary colour has one that is said to be 'complementary' to it, created by mixing the other two primary colours (purple, for example, is the complementary of yellow). Using complement colours is always effective in a painting (think of red poppies in a green field), Colours in the same part of the spectrum (blues and greens, reds and oranges) are said to be 'harmonious' and generally evoke a calm mood, while colours on opposite sides of the wheel are 'contrasting' colours which, if used carefully, can make a painting seem more dynamic. Don't worry too much about the theory: the best way to learn about colours is simply to use them and then try to analyse the effect and mood they create.

1
2
3
4
5
6
7
8
9
10

Colour tonal value chart *Making colour tonal value charts in a range of different colours is a very useful practice exercise, as it will help you improve your control of colours and tones. Follow the instructions given on page 18.*

Pumpkin field by Jane Hughes

When drawing a landscape, the most significant element is the physical space. In a portrait or still life, the space is quite shallow, sometimes no more than 30–60 cm (1–2 feet), but in a landscape it may extend as far as the eye can see, and it is important to find ways of conveying this sense of recession. Far-away features in the picture appear less distinct than closer objects, due to tiny specks of dust in the atmosphere that create a progressively hazy effect, known as aerial perspective. When working with a medium such as coloured pencils, you can emphasise this characteristic by drawing loosely in the background, with the more detailed work restricted to the foreground.

Practice points

- WORKING QUICKLY AND FREELY
- COLOUR AND TEXTURE WITH COLOURED PENCILS
- CREATING SPACE AND RECESSION

STAGE 1

THE FRAMEWORK

■ This field of pumpkins is very flat, stretching away towards the distant mountains and separated from them by the tall crops in the field beyond. Since there are few other outstanding features, apart from the rather unexciting sheds, the pumpkins will form the main focus of interest in the picture.

Trust your eye to measure the position of the field edges and the outline of the mountains; this is to be a free sketch, so don't labour the drawing at this stage.

Set the composition on the page, working lightly with a green-grey pencil.

Lightly draw in the large shed near the centre, using a dull red.

Mark the position of the nearest pumpkin, using a light orange pencil.

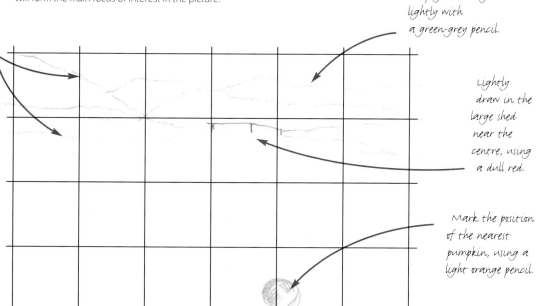

STAGE 2
BUILD ON THE FRAMEWORK

■ The diminishing size of the pumpkins as they recede into the distance helps to define the space in this sketch. Having marked the position of the nearest pumpkin, draw in the farthest one you can see above it, very lightly, judging its size against the first one. This is not a precise measurement, but it sets the range of sizes for the fruits, which will reduce visually in perspective towards the far side of the field. Be selective; it is not necessary to try to draw every single pumpkin.

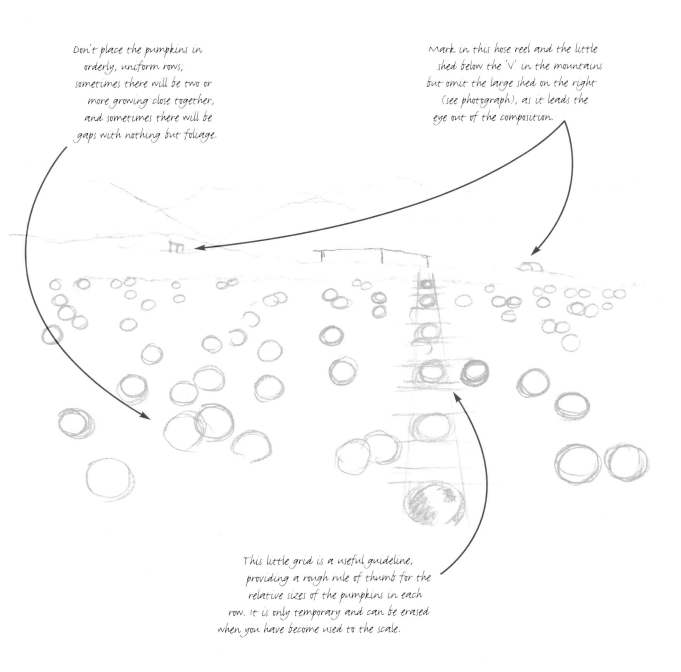

Don't place the pumpkins in orderly, uniform rows; sometimes there will be two or more growing close together, and sometimes there will be gaps with nothing but foliage.

Mark in this hose reel and the little shed below the 'V' in the mountains but omit the large shed on the right (see photograph), as it leads the eye out of the composition.

This little grid is a useful guideline, providing a rough rule of thumb for the relative sizes of the pumpkins in each row. It is only temporary and can be erased when you have become used to the scale.

STAGE 3
DESCRIPTIVE COLOUR

■ With the position of most of the pumpkins plotted out, the sketch is ready for some more descriptive colour to help clarify the composition. The far edge of the field is marked by its border with the neighbouring crop, which is about the darkest part of the picture. The mountains beyond are defined by subtle changes of colour from stronger to lighter as they recede in layers into the background sky.

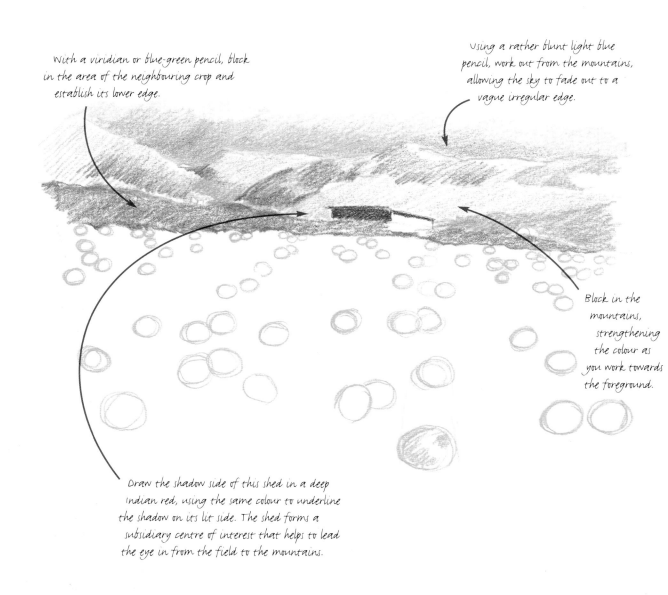

With a viridian or blue-green pencil, block in the area of the neighbouring crop and establish its lower edge.

Using a rather blunt light blue pencil, work out from the mountains, allowing the sky to fade out to a vague irregular edge.

Block in the mountains, strengthening the colour as you work towards the foreground.

Draw the shadow side of this shed in a deep Indian red, using the same colour to underline the shadow on its lit side. The shed forms a subsidiary centre of interest that helps to lead the eye in from the field to the mountains.

STAGE 4
DEVELOP TEXTURE AND TONE

■ The mass of bold, deep-cut leaves makes a rich texture, punctuated by the orange globes of the fruit. Despite the complexity of the mass of leaves and stems, the overall appearance of the field is remarkably even. The texture is quite broken at the front of the field, becoming more generalised towards the distance.

With a blunted light-green pencil, block in colour across the far side of the field. Work over the stems and around the pumpkins, drawing leaf edges to overlap some of them.

Use a yellowish pale green to draw the stems, pressing hard to indent the paper. Try to relate the stems to the pumpkins, but don't worry if they seem a bit random.

As you work towards the foreground, the leaf shapes appear larger and more separate, allowing the ground beneath to show through. Use a deeper green to describe the undulating forms, particularly the plants where the edge of the picture peters out.

Begin to colour the pumpkins themselves at this stage, so that you develop the fruit and leaves together. Use a pale gold-orange as a base, overlaying it with deeper orange to build the rounded shapes.

STAGE 5
FILL IN THE GAPS

■ The main features of the composition are now in place, so you can add a little more loosely drawn detail to give coherence to the distant view and the crop in the neighbouring field. The remaining areas of ground showing through between the pumpkin plants are not of great interest, being covered with a mass of weeds, so invent some areas of weed-free brown earth to fill in the gaps and make more of the pumpkins in the foreground.

Make stippled and dotted strokes in deeper greens to point up the rows of this tall, leafy crop, then slightly build up the colours of the shed and hose reel with brick red and blue and grey respectively.

To suggest the distant forested slopes, make soft, scribbly marks in ochres, greens and browns.

Work over the blocked-in area of pumpkin greenery, breaking it up a little with deeper greens to give an impression of the massed leaves.

Where the plants are spread apart in the foreground, make some roughly drawn marks to suggest broken soil and then work over these with deep violet in the shadows of the plants.

Using a blunted pencil, soften and slightly darken the edges of the mountains with deep red-violet, then blend the sky and the farthest mountains a little by working over them with white.

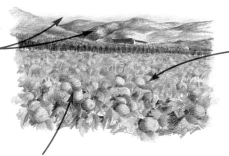

Intensify the colour and shadows of the pumpkins across the field. Remember that warm, light colours advance while cool, dark colours recede.

Use both red-violet and blue-violet to strengthen shadow detail, making the most of the effect of complementary colours.

Build up the detail in the closest groups of pumpkins, but don't overdo it—the detail should be an accent rather than a major statement.

STAGE 6
FINAL ADJUSTMENTS

■ Although there is some fairly complicated subject matter in this sketch, it is very simple in compositional terms. Generalising the 'busy' areas of the middleground and background slightly and bringing more colour and detail into the large foreground area ensure that space and distance remain important, while the foreground is lively and interesting.

Poppy field by Barry Freeman

There can be few more enticing landscape subjects than a field full of poppies in full flower. A natural complementary contrast is provided by the red of the flowers set against the greens of surrounding fields and hills. Oil pastel is an excellent medium for such a subject, as rich, deep colours can be built up very quickly by using heavy pressure on the sticks. But in this case the artist has decided to work relatively lightly, using a higher colour 'key' to suggest sunlight rather than reproducing the rather dark, heavy colours in the photograph. He is working on pastel paper, and has let the paper show through the pastel strokes in places to enhance the light, airy effect.

Practice points

- **DECIDING ON A COLOUR KEY**
- **SUGGESTING LIGHT**
- **USING OIL PASTEL**
- **VARYING THE PRESSURE**

STAGE 1

BLOCK IN THE MAIN SHAPES

■ Use a charcoal pencil or a stick of willow charcoal to sketch in the main lines of the composition, keeping detail to a minimum. Then add colour to the sky and fields, keeping the pastel strokes light so that the paper shows through.

You can make the charcoal line fairly heavy here, as the line of trees will be one of the darkest tones in the picture, and the strong line will emphasise the shape.

Keep the colours relatively cool in the background, using cobalt blue as an undercolour for the more distant fields and pale blue-green for the nearer one, above the trees.

Keep the direction of the light in mind, and shade the dark sides of the trees with indigo, using the pastel slightly more heavily, but making sure you do not overfill the grain of the paper.

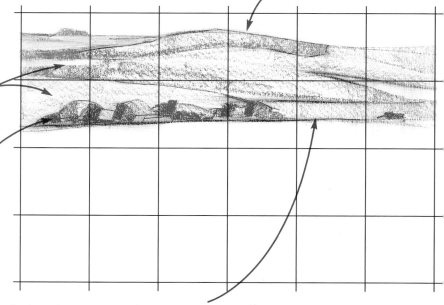

Carefully place the dividing line between foreground and background, and avoid splitting the composition in half. Here the poppy field is given two-thirds of the picture space.

STAGE 2
ESTABLISH THE COLOURS
■ Work on the foreground next, before adding any further tones and colours to the background. Once you have the main colour framework in place, with all of the paper lightly covered, you can begin to see the picture emerging.

Now that you have warmer greens in place in the foreground field, this green looks cooler and bluer by contrast and is thus pushed back in space.

Use the pastel sticks on their sides to make broad strokes of pale yellow-green to indicate the grass between the flowers. Make the colour slightly darker towards the front of the picture.

Use the side of a red-orange pastel stick to suggest the poppies, but make shorter strokes than those used for the grass and vary the pressure from light to medium.

STAGE 3
BUILD UP THE COLOUR

■ The field of poppies is the central theme of the picture, so you need to build up the colours in this area and those on the middle-ground trees before returning to fields and hills in the background.

Lay a mid-tone olive green over the indigo to warm the sunlit sides of the trees, using fairly light pressure.

After defining the middle-ground trees, you can begin to strengthen the pattern of the background fields, laying on the same mid-tone olive green.

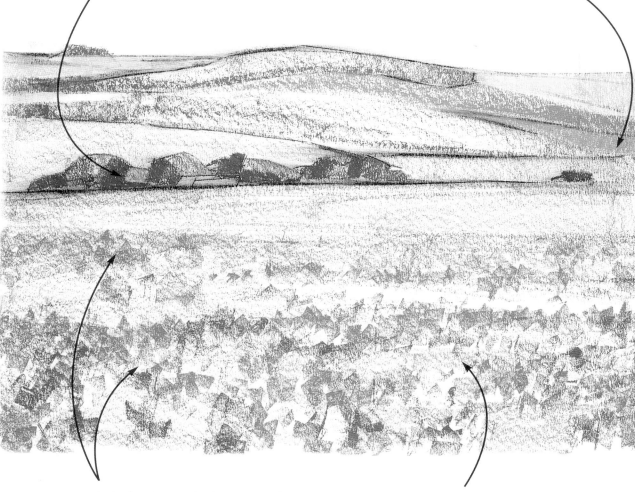

Apply the red-orange loosely to suggest the clumps of poppies, making the marks smaller towards the back of the field. Strengthen the colours along the tops with oranges and yellows, putting in touches of pink to suggest the fall of light.

Use the same yellow-greens as before for the grass, but increase the pressure to build up the depth of colour.

STAGE 4
BALANCE THE TONES

■ In a painting like this, where colour and light are all-important, the dark tones need to be placed with care. Too many dark areas could destroy the effect, but it is essential to have some, as they give structure to the composition and prevent it from looking too bland.

These tree shapes echo those of the middleground trees in both shape and tone, though they are slightly paler and much bluer in colour.

To maintain the red/green complementary colour theme, use orange-red overlaid with pale blue for the barn roofs. This is more harmonious than the stark white seen in the photograph.

Use light oranges and pinks for the distant poppies, as the tones here are paler than those in the foreground.

Build up the tonal contrasts in the poppy field with stronger reds, and suggest the shapes by varying the pastel marks.

STAGE 5
INCREASE THE CONTRASTS

■ At this stage, when all the main elements of the composition are in place, you can consider how much more contrast is needed and whether some foreground detail would give the picture more punch.

For the grass in the middle distance, make long strokes of yellow-green, applying medium pressure. This vivid colour enhances the sunlit effect, and contrasts with the blue-greens of the background fields and hills.

To help the reds of the poppies to stand out, darken the greens, using a mid-tone grey-green for the areas of grass in between the flowers. Do not make these 'negative shapes' too uniform in size.

In the foreground, apply olive green firmly, taking the colour around the sunlit edges of some of the flowers to suggest their shapes without being too tight and fussy. This warm green, together with the small marks of deep red, pushes the cooler colours back in space to help create the illusion of recession.

Using diagonal strokes to contrast with the horizontals below, stroke on varying greens, blues and greys to heighten the contrast.

Fill in the distant clump of trees more solidly with blue-grey, and work yellow ochre over it for the larger trees above the field.

Lay a pale warm grey all over the field to alter the tone and help the area to recede.

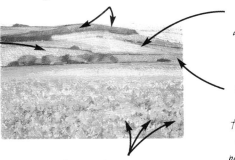

Suggest the 'stripes' of the field with the tip of a blue-green pastel stick.

Add yellows to the grass between the poppies, and darken some of the flowers with a deeper red than those used previously.

STAGE 6
FINAL TOUCHES

■ It is not always easy to know when a picture is finished, so if you are not sure, put the work away for a while and then come back to it with a fresh eye. The artist has decided to enhance the sense of space by making some adjustments to the tones and colours in the background and by adding more colour and contrast to the poppy field.

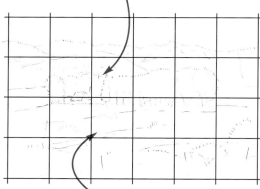

EXERCISE 8

Red cliffs by Moira Clinch

The soft, late-afternoon October sunlight gave the landscape an attractive delicacy well suited to a line-and-wash treatment. The artist has used pencil for the line rather than the more usual pen and ink, as this gives a softer effect as well as enabling her to build up tones before applying the washes. The fading colours of the foliage in the scrubland and on the trees blend gently into the grey pencil tones used for the tree tops and twiggy sage bushes. The red of the hills has been deliberately toned down to prevent them coming forwards and destroying the sense of space.

Practice points

- **ADJUSTING PENCIL TONES AND DETAILS**
- **LAYING WASHES OVER PENCIL**
- **USING AERIAL PERSPECTIVE**

STAGE 1

START THE DRAWING

■ To help you position the various elements in the composition, divide your paper into equal sections – you can either draw light grid lines or simply imagine the divisions. Sketch in the main features in line initially, and don't begin shading until you are satisfied with the composition and perspective. Then begin to build up the tones, using a 6B pencil and working from the top down to prevent smudging. As you will be building up the drawing in a series of stages, there is a danger of grease from your hand forming a water-repellent layer which would make it difficult to apply the washes cleanly, so rest your drawing hand on a clean piece of paper. When drawing the distant tree-clad mountains, bear in mind the effect of aerial perspective, which makes tones lighter in the distance, with less contrast.

To position the trees, make small marks in the direction of the branches rather than drawing the whole outline, as this allows you to make adjustments more easily. An outline could mark the paper even if you are using a light pressure.

Block in the dark coniferous trees on the mountain tops as small triangles of varying shape and size.

To create a realistic perspective effect, dot in a few trees to appear as though they are just over the crest of the mountain, and make those on the lower and nearer slopes larger.

If you wish you can make changes in this area. The artist has removed some of the scrub in order to see slightly more of the track and fencing.

Hatch in the simple areas with diagonal strokes, but take care not to make them too dark or to introduce too much contrast. These tree-clad mountains must appear to be in the distance.

STAGE 2
THE FOCAL POINT

■ The main centre of interest is the line of trees and farm buildings, with the mountains forming a dark backdrop for the light branches and leaves, and the tall conifers contrasting with the lighter tones of the buildings. At this stage render the group in medium tones, drawing in the tree trunks, branches and buildings. Once you are happy with the positioning, you can begin to analyse the tones.

Start adding some shadows, but don't worry if they are not dark enough; you will be adjusting tones throughout the drawing, and can return to this area after working on the foreground.

Use horizontal marks for the conifers to give the impression of the layers.

Draw the branches as though radiating out from the centre.

STAGE 3
BUILD UP TONE AND DETAIL

■ Now work over the whole of the drawing, adding detail and strengthening tones where needed. The light is coming from the right, so concentrate the darker shadows on the left sides of the trees and buildings to give form.

Strengthen the cast shadows under the trees.

Draw in the strata and fault lines, noticing how the horizontal lines slip down at the faults.

Look carefully at the scrubland and analyse the shapes and patterns made by the jumbled bushes. Draw in little overlapping hummocks for the sage bush; shade in the base of each hummock so that the top edge is highlighted against the bush behind.

Draw in the fence; this plays an important part in the composition, as it leads the eye in towards the other fence and the buildings behind it.

STAGE 4
LAY THE FIRST WASHES

■ In this drawing, the pencil provides the structure and linear detail, while the watercolour washes accentuate the sense of space and distance as well as adding colour and atmosphere.

For the sunlit areas of the trees, use a stronger mix, mainly of cadmium yellow.

Mix a very dilute solution of cadmium yellow and yellow ochre, wash it over the whole of the foreground and middlegound, and leave it to dry.

Don't worry if the wash is not flat, as small variations will enhance the impression of freshness and spontaneity.

Mix a weak wash of cerulean blue and cobalt blue for the sky area, and paint this same colour over the tree-clad areas of the mountains to make these distant areas fade gently into the sky.

STAGE 5
STRENGTHEN THE TONES

■ At this stage you can alternate between drawing and painting; line-and-wash drawings are usually more successful if the two processes are not seen as separate. But make sure that the paint is thoroughly dry before drawing on top.

Add a wash of light red to the cliffs; this will be the highlight colour.

Knock back some of the pencil detail by adding vertical hatching to some of the areas; this has the effect of linking and softening the details.

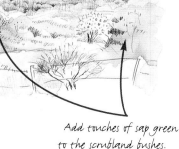

Draw in more detail in the foreground, indicating bushes, twigs and dead flower heads.

Add touches of sap green to the scrubland bushes.

STAGE 6
FINAL ADJUSTMENTS

■ Continue to add stronger touches of colour and detailed pencil work throughout the drawing. As the shapes are organic, you can have some fun and paint either wet-on-dry or wet-in-wet (or both), as it doesn't really matter if colours bleed into each other or if a wash dries with a hard edge. Let the paint dry thoroughly, and then add final pencil details to complete the scene.

Mix French ultramarine and sap green for the distant coniferous forest, paint a wash layer and add some tiny tree shapes that bleed into the shadows. You can also use this mix for the cast shadows under the main trees and house.

Paint the roof of the house with dilute viridian, and the walls with a mix of yellow ocher and light red.

Add touches of sap green to the trees.

To make the pale hazy tops of the trees stand out, make sure you have painted the scene through the base of the trees.

Build up the strata of the hills with successive layers of light red.

Using various mixes of yellow ochre, light red, and sap green, wash in the shapes of the foreground shrubs and trees over the structural pencil lines.

Perspective

Many beginners believe that landscapes are easier to draw than urban scenes, because you don't have to cope with perspective. But although perspective effects are less complex in landscape, it is important to understand the basic rules. Otherwise you won't be able to make your sketches appear three-dimensional.

Simple linear perspective

The concept of perspective is based on the optical illusion that receding parallel lines converge, finally meeting at a point on what is known as the horizon line, which is your own eye level. Objects become smaller and smaller towards this horizon line, so if you had three trees of a similar size placed at different distances from you, the nearest one clearly would be the largest. You can observe these effects for yourself without knowing the rules, but it is less easy to make mistakes if you understand the principles. It is often hard to appreciate how small, for example, a distant field is, because your knowledge tells you that it's actually the same size as one in the foreground.

If you have problems with relative sizes, take measurements by holding a pencil up at arm's length and sliding your thumb up and down it. It is also helpful to mark in the horizon (eye-level) line when you begin to draw, so that you can make the perspective consistent. If you have to change position as you draw, perhaps sitting down if you began standing up, the horizon line will change with you, which can be confusing if you have not established it clearly.

The pencil test
Your brain may think that your eyes are deceiving you. To measure objects, hold a pencil at arm's length and slide your thumb up and down the pencil.

Tree-lined road
A classic example of linear one-point perspective, where the receding trees meet at the horizon line in the lower half of the drawing.

Aerial perspective

Reductions of tone (shown to the right) are due to another kind of perspective, known as aerial, atmospheric or colour perspective. This is very important in landscape painting, as it is the primary means of creating the illusion of space. Tiny specks of dust in the atmosphere cause colours and tones to become paler in the distance, and objects have very little distinguishable detail. The colours also become 'cooler', with more blues, greys, and blue-greens. To take an example of three trees in different parts of the picture place, the one in the foreground will show strong contrasts of tone, and warmer, yellower greens; that in the middleground will veer toward blue and be lighter in tone; and the distant tree will be paler and bluer still.

Mountain view
The effects of aerial perspective, which makes colours appear paler and bluer towards the distance, are very clearly seen in an expansive landscape like this.

Artistic licence

Any of these perspective effects can be exaggerated to make more dynamic compositions and colour schemes. You can bring in warmer colours than you actually see, such as reds and oranges, in the foreground in order to bring it forwards in space and push the distant areas farther away. You can increase the width of a road or river in the foreground, artificially narrowing it as it recedes, or you can give extra height to a foreground feature such as a fence. Artistic devices such as these can make a drawing or painting more exciting by giving the sense of depth and the feeling that the viewer can 'walk into' the scene portrayed.

Using artistic license *Objects become smaller the nearer they are to the horizon line. The diminishing patchwork of vineyards, and the receding road, have been exaggerated slightly to draw the eye into the distance.*

EXERCISE 9

Snowy lane by Jim Woods

Snow is always a beguiling subject, especially when lit by sunshine, as the snow reflects the blue of the sky, creating lovely blue or violet shadows. In this case, the warm browns and yellows of the trees contrast excitingly with the snow shadows to make a simple but attractive colour scheme. The artist is working from a photograph, which he took as a precaution, knowing the snow was unlikely to last long enough to be painted. He has made a more lively pattern than that seen in the photo by taking the sunlit patches right across the lane instead of concentrating most of the shadow in one place.

Practice points
- COMBINING WATERCOLOUR AND PENCIL
- REPEATING COLOURS
- INCLUDING A FIGURE
- OBSERVING PERSPECTIVE EFFECTS

For this area, use a mid-toned mix of cobalt blue and indigo, warmed with touches of burnt sienna and raw sienna.

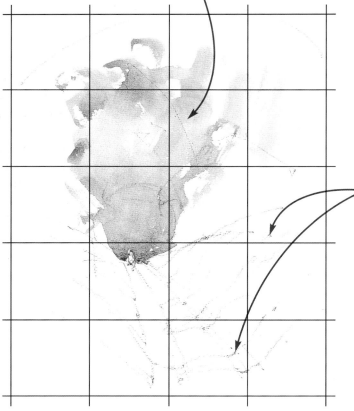

STAGE 1
FIRST STAGES

■ Start by making a drawing with carbon pencil, sketching in the shadows and the main tree masses, but not the tree trunks, which are to be left until later. Take care with the converging perspective lines of the banks and lane, as it is important to get these right. Then block in the area at the end of the lane with a blue-grey watercolour wash.

It is important to draw the shadows accurately, as they delineate the shape of the lane and the banks. You may find it helpful to start with a series of small dots at the top of the right banks and the edges of the lane.

STAGE 2
ESTABLISHING THE COLOURS

■ The colour scheme is a simple one, based on the contrast of cool blues and warm browns and yellows, so keep your palette as simple as possible and try to repeat the same colours from area to area as well as using the same basic colours in mixtures. This helps to unify the composition.

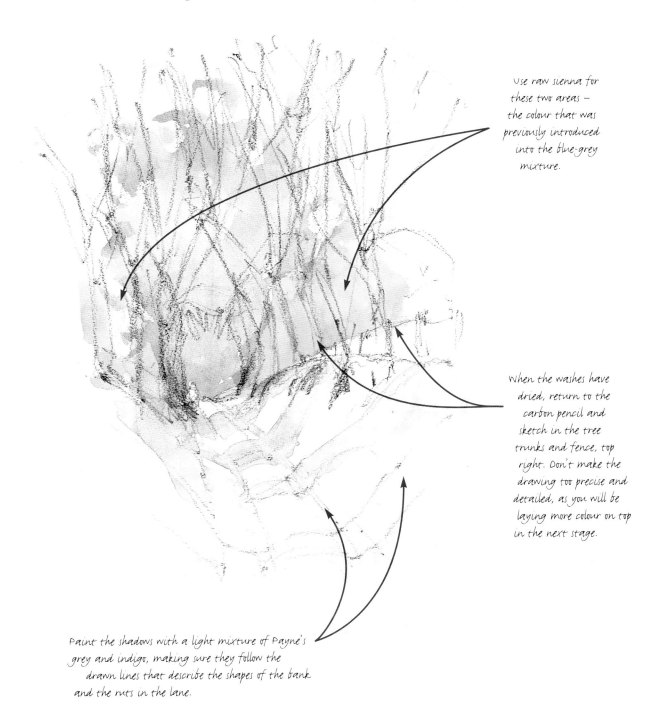

Use raw sienna for these two areas – the colour that was previously introduced into the blue-grey mixture.

When the washes have dried, return to the carbon pencil and sketch in the tree trunks and fence, top right. Don't make the drawing too precise and detailed, as you will be laying more colour on top in the next stage.

Paint the shadows with a light mixture of Payne's grey and indigo, making sure they follow the drawn lines that describe the shapes of the bank and the ruts in the lane.

STAGE 3
STRENGTHENING THE COLOUR

■ The next stage is to block in the tops of the trees, using mixtures of burnt umber and burnt sienna, with a little ultramarine blue added here and there. When the paint has dried, reinforce the drawing where necessary, again using the carbon pencil.

Use a large round brush and let it follow the direction of the clumps of small twigs, leaving areas of white paper between them in places. Drop in small touches of blue made from Payne's grey and indigo, wet-in-wet.

Paint in the tree trunks with stronger mixtures of the same colours; when they are dry, draw over them to give them more definition.

With a small round brush, sketch in the small branches, working from the bottom upwards and lifting the brush slightly so that the brushstrokes become progressively narrower, coming to a point at the top.

At the end of the lane, the brown mixtures have been laid over the first wash of blue-grey, making the color cooler and thus helping the sense of recession.

STAGE 4
MAKING A FOCAL POINT

■ Although paintings should always be well planned at the outset, you will continue to make decisions throughout the painting process, and sometimes right at the end of it. The artist came back to the picture after a short break and decided to include a red-clad figure at the end of the lane to create a strong focal point. He also introduced some warm colours into the foreground to make the contrasts less stark.

The placing of the figure, together with the perspective lines, ensures that the eye travels into the picture towards the end of the lane. When painting a distant figure, avoid detail. Identify the main shape, and try to use no more than one or two dabs of the brush.

Do a little more drawing with the carbon pencil to emphasise the focal point, and add further drawing wherever necessary – but don't overdo it.

strengthen these areas with more raw sienna; when dry, add some touches of definition with burnt sienna.

Using a very pale mixture of burnt umber with a touch of alizarin crimson, wash over parts of the lane and banks, taking some of this new colour over the blue-grey of the shadows. This warm colour makes a link with the trees, tying the two areas together.

THE FUNDAMENTALS

Composition

However well you can draw, your drawings and paintings will not succeed completely unless you think about how to compose them. A sketch with a dominant feature placed right in the middle is usually very dull, failing to engage the viewer's attention. Always try to create a rhythm in the composition that leads the eye into and around the picture, and create interest by varying shapes and balancing tones.

Preliminary decisions

When you are sketching outdoors you can move around to choose the best viewpoint, which is the first step in deciding on the composition. Using a viewfinder (a piece of cardboard with a rectangular hole cut in it)

is very helpful in making these first decisions, and you can hold it up at different distances from your eye to experiment with different skylines, more sky or more foreground. If you have time to visit the scene more than once before sketching, choose different times of day, as you may find that a different light source, perhaps with more dramatic shadows, improves the composition.

Composing the picture

Although there are no set rules for composition, there are some useful tips. The focal point in a landscape is usually placed in the middle distance, but avoid putting it right in the centre of the picture, and think of ways to lead the eye towards it. These could be the diagonal lines of a foreground field or a path curving in from the foreground. Also, make the contrasts of tone or colour strongest at the centre of interest, as this automatically draws the eye. Don't concentrate all the attention on this focal point, leaving dull areas elsewhere where nothing is happening. However, bear in mind that cropping the design around a centre of interest can often be

Using a viewfinder
Experiment with a viewfinder to find the most interesting scene to sketch. Your first viewpoint will not necessarily be the best, and sketches of landscapes don't always need to be 'horizontal'. Try a portrait format once in a while.

A field in winter
The track in the foreground leads the eye to the large tree just off centre, and then beyond to the next group of trees. These trees hold the composition together.

effective, especially when working from photographs.

Vary the shapes, contrasting squares or rectangles with round shapes and curves, and don't repeat exactly the same shape in any one area. Distant trees, for example, may appear as little more than rounded blobs, but they are not all uniform. If the composition is mainly horizontal, as in a landscape with fields, putting in a vertical object such as a tree or fence post will hold it together.

Working from photographs

If using reference photos, beware of copying them exactly; any number of details can be altered to make a good composition without detracting from the original subject matter. For example, the sky or the foliage can be changed to suggest different weather or time of day; you can alter the light source, bringing in shadows and stronger tonal contrasts; and you can omit unhelpful features and make more of others. Don't automatically stick to the same format, either. You might make an upright composition from a horizontal photograph by leaving out dull areas at the sides or by increasing the foreground and sky. Think of the photograph as a starting point for the ultimate aim of making the picture work.

Working from a photo *Photographs can be useful reference tools and a starting point for a composition. Rather than copying a scene, use artistic licence to make the composition more interesting.*

EXERCISE 10

Waterfall by Janet Whittle

When you are working from a photograph there is always a tendency to copy it directly, using the same composition and putting in every single feature. But this does not often result in a good drawing. The artist has taken the photo as her starting point, making several rough sketches to work out the composition.

<table>
<tr><td>Practice points</td></tr>
<tr><td>• WORKING OUT THE COMPOSITION</td></tr>
<tr><td>• BALANCING TONES</td></tr>
<tr><td>• DECIDING WHAT TO LEAVE OUT</td></tr>
</table>

She has decided to crop in a little to make more of the water and to simplify the rocks, thus giving more emphasis to the waterfall, which is the natural focal point.

The high placing of the waterfall ensures that it catches attention as the focal point of the drawing.

The tree trunks are to be left as light against dark, so draw them in lightly as a guide for the subsequent shading.

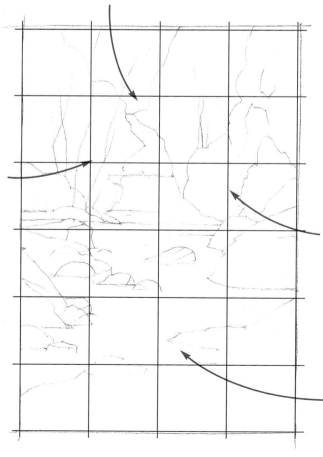

STAGE 1

ESTABLISH THE MAIN FEATURES

■ In a monochrome drawing, tone is all-important, and the success of the composition relies on achieving a good balance of darks and lights, so think about tone from the outset, even though you will be using line only for the initial drawing.

This area can be simplified into areas of mid- to dark tone, with little detail.

The artist added more water to make a feature of a reflection from the large rock, and she has omitted the log seen in the photo.

suggest the foliage against the sky with small marks going in different directions.

Leave white paper for the tree trunks and for occasional clumps of foliage.

STAGE 2
ADD TONE

■ To avoid smudging completed areas, begin shading in the top left of the paper, working over to the right and leaving highlight areas such as the tree trunks and waterfall as white paper. If you are left-handed, reverse the procedure, working from right to left.

shade the woodland and rocks on the right with an HB pencil, varying the strokes and leaving white paper at the top of the small bush and rock.

With short vertical strokes, put in the steps of the waterfall, keeping the top edge soft and varying the bottom edges to suggest foam on the water.

STEP 3
DEEPEN THE TONES

■ It may be tempting to start working on the foreground at this stage – the large area of white paper seems to invite you to fill it in – but it is better to establish the tonal structure at the top of the picture first.

Again with the 3B, put a second tone on the foliage, leaving some of the first tone showing. To suggest recession, make the clumps of foliage smaller towards the background.

Using a 3B pencil, put in a dark tone behind the background tree trunks and clump of light foliage, and shade the trunks under these slightly.

Leave the small tree mainly as the first tone, darkening the tone behind the trunk to emphasise it.

Once the tones of the trees are in place, you will have a key against which to judge the tones needed for the rocks. Shade the shadowed sides fairly heavily with the 3B pencil.

STAGE 4
MIDDLEGROUND AND FOREGROUND

■ Now give the drawing an overall, coherent pattern, repeating on the water the combination of mid- and dark tones used for the trees.

Using the HB pencil, lay a first tone on the rocks, darkening in places with the 3B. Make small, dark squiggly marks to suggest the encrusted surface.

Darken the shadowed areas of water with horizontal lines using a 3B pencil.

Shade in the water with horizontal strokes made with the HB pencil, leaving some light areas at the bottom of the waterfall and adding ripples as you work forwards.

Suggest the texture of the foreground grass with upright diagonal strokes made with the HB pencil. Keep the strokes shorter towards the back of the area.

STAGE 5
PUT IT ALL TOGETHER
■ Darken the tones in a few places and work more on the foreground and water to make them as complete as the trees.

Use the 3B pencil to put in some dark foliage in the background. Then blend it with the HB pencil to soften it.

Put in some ripples and rock reflections. Use the tip of the 3B pencil (well sharpened) to make occasional sharp lines at the edges.

Shade the steps of the waterfall with the HB pencil, keeping the tone as light as possible, as it is vital that this reads as a pale shape against the dark of the trees.

This large rock needs a strong reflection to contrast with the light areas of grass below, so use a 9B pencil to make vertical strokes.

Put in more tone on the foreground grass to balance the trees, making strokes that follow the direction of the clumps of grass.

EXERCISE **11**

Pond and hawthorn bush
by Janet Whittle

It is wise to have your camera with you at all times; you may see a good subject at any point in the day, even when you are simply going shopping or collecting the children from school. This scene, with the hawthorn in full bloom complemented by the buttercups in the field beyond, was one that the artist happened upon more or less by accident, but she felt that it was too good to miss, and she took several reference photos as well as making a quick sketch. She has made several compositional changes to the final picture, notably increasing the slope of the field and hills, exaggerating the reflection, and simplifying the large tree so that it forms a more defined shape that contrasts with the hawthorn.

Practice points
- **WORKING WITH PASTEL**
- **PAINTING REFLECTIONS**
- **COMPOSING THE PICTURE**
- **ADDING COLOUR ACCENTS**

STAGE 1
CHOOSE YOUR COMPOSITION

■ Take a number of reference photographs from different angles, so that you can choose a composition that inspires you. Although the subject is the same, the focal points in these photographs are different: the hawthorn bush is dominant in one, in another the water takes precedence.

The artist chose a view with the hawthorn bush slightly off-centre, because she felt this made a more interesting composition.

The artist included some foreground foliage from another photograph to balance the sketch.

The view behind the main bushes adds depth to the sketch, so this was included in the final work.

STAGE 2
THE FRAMEWORK

■ The special papers sold for pastel work are coloured rather than white, and the choice of colour is important, as it will influence the pastel colours laid over it. In some pastel paintings, small patches of the paper are deliberately left showing to stand as a colour in their own right. Here the pastel has been rubbed well into the paper, but although the underlying colour is only just visible in a few places, it gives a warm glow to the work, whereas a blue or grey paper would produce a cooler effect overall.

Working on a light ochre-coloured paper, draw the main lines of the composition with a pastel pencil just a shade or two darker. Do not use graphite pencil for the drawing, as it is slightly greasy and is difficult to cover with pastel colour.

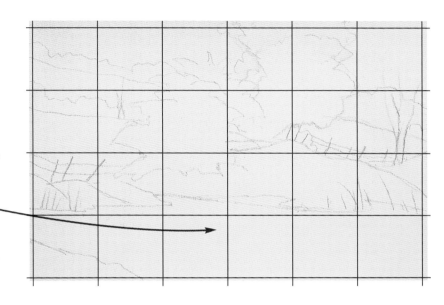

Start at the top of the sky, using a pale-blue pastel and blending it into the paper colour towards the bottom by rubbing with a finger.

Lay in the background bushes with a darker, more purplish blue, blend in, and then use the sky colour again to pick out the light sides. For the fields, use a light greenish blue.

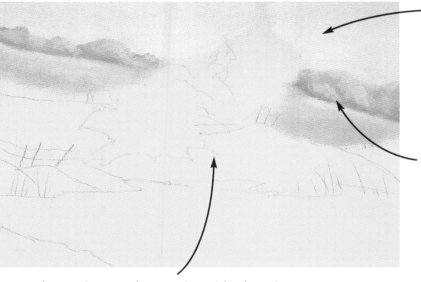

Reserve the central area as the paper colour. Although pastel is opaque, and colours can be laid one over another, it is best to avoid too heavy a build-up of colour, as this will clog the paper.

STAGE 3
BUILD UP THE TONES

■ Now you can begin to add some really dark tones to give structure to the composition. One of the joys of pastel painting is that light colours can be laid over dark ones, so you need not be nervous about making the tones too dark. However, pale colours can lose some of their clarity and become muddy if laid over very dark ones, so continue to reserve the area where the hawthorn bush is to go.

With a very dark green pastel, lay in the whole shape of the right-hand tree, and then use a slightly lighter shade to indicate the highlights on the foliage clumps.

The background tree is more blue and lighter in tone because it is more distant, so use a mid-tone blue-green for this and the hedgerow, again lightening some of the clumps with a paler shade.

Paint the fields with two shades of a strong yellowish green, making them darker at the top and bringing in a little of the darker tone in the bottom right, where they meet the dark green of the pond bank.

STAGE 4
WORK ON THE DETAIL

■ Before working on the hawthorn bush, which is the focal point of the picture, adjust the tones of the tree behind it and put in the right-hand tree and the fences. These details could be left until last, but there is a risk of smudging if you try to work on middleground areas after the foreground has been filled in.

The light is coming from the right, so concentrate the lighter greens on that side. Take some of the sky colour into and around the clumps of foliage and put in touches of very light creamy yellow in the bottom right to reinforce the sunlit effect.

Start the hawthorn bush in the same way as the dark tree, but don't cover it completely with the green. For the blossom, use a very pale pink and touches of mid-tone pink on the sunlit side. Choose a pale blue for the shadowed areas, varying the size of the pastel marks to suggest that some areas are coming towards you and others receding.

Put in the smaller tree on the right, using the same greens as for the background tree. Leave gaps between the clumps of foliage and run the dark brown branches between them.

STAGE 5
PULL IT TOGETHER

■ Now you can begin on the foreground, starting with the reflections. These play a major role in the composition, providing strong verticals that lead the eye up to the focal point.

The contrasts of both tone and texture give an extra punch to this central area of the drawing.

The buttercups are too distant to be seen clearly, so just suggest them lightly with a yellow slightly paler in tone than the green. To avoid smudging the foreground, hold your hand away from the paper; these marks do not need to be controlled and precise.

Use the same colours for the reflections as for the landscape features, but make vertical strokes, blending the colours with a finger to give a soft effect.

Indicate the reeds and grasses on the bank with light strokes of mid-green made with the tip of the pastel stick, and make a few small flower-shaped blobs with the blossom colours.

STAGE 6
FINAL ACCENTS AND DETAILS

■ The final stages of a sketch – when you can put in the small colour accents and highlights that bring it to life – are very enjoyable, but it is easy to overwork a piece unless you think carefully about what you are doing. If you are not sure how much still needs to be done, put the work away for an hour or two and return to it with a fresh eye.

JANET WHITTLE

It is often necessary to exercise a little artistic licence when sketching reflections, because these give the impression of a vertical surface rather than a horizontal one. Suggest a few ripples to explain the surface.

Lay in small accents of deep yellow on the side of the tree and add a few more flowers on the pond bank to give more sparkle to the tree and enhance the sunlit feel of the landscape.

This area needs to come forwards, so put in some flowers and foliage, working these bright colour accents over the deep green.

FOCUS on Landscapes

Once you have mastered the fundamentals, you may wish to concentrate on subject areas that are specific to landscapes – for example, Trees and Skies, or Shadows and Reflections. Simple step-by-step exercises show how to perfect all those details that will set your sketch apart.

FOCUS ON LANDSCAPES

Trees and skies

When drawing skies, you don't need to reproduce every cloud in minute detail, but you do want to give an impression of the weather conditions, as this will give a sense of atmosphere to the work. The situation is similar with trees: unless you are really close, you need not engage with botanical detail, but you do want to give an idea of the type of tree. So look for the main shapes and forms first, as these give vital clues to the species and maturity of the tree. An oak tree has a very different profile to that of a conifer or silver birch, and young saplings have a different skeleton from more mature trees.

Tree identifier
Trees grow in a variety of different shapes and colours.

Pine

Weeping willow

Cyprus

Conifer

Beech

Chestnut

Drawing and sketching trees

Foliage colours are also an important factor in helping the viewer to identify the trees and give you the opportunity to add interest to your sketch. The colours will vary from blue-greens to yellow-greens and from dark to light – and from yellows to oranges and reds in the autumn. Even in an area perceived initially just as green you can interpret the colours, bringing in blues, yellows and purples. Tree trunks and branches are rarely brown; they can be grey, green, and even red, depending both on the species of tree and on the lighting conditions.

In summer you will only see glimpses of trunks and branches, so it can be difficult to understand their relationship with the foliage, but in winter you can clearly see the structure of trees, so this is the time to observe, draw, and acquire the knowledge that will make your subsequent drawing better and more confident.

To add twigs and small branches, a long slender pointed sable paintbrush called a rigger brush is useful. This has longer hairs than a normal brush and holds more paint, so you don't have to keep refilling it.

Drawing and sketching skies

In a monochrome drawing, skies can often be left as white paper, perhaps with a light suggestion of a few clouds, but if you are using any of the colour media, give the sky more thought. A good general rule is to avoid detail in the sky if you want to focus attention on the land, for example, in a painting

Rigger brush
Use a rigger brush to sketch delicate branches, twigs and leaves in watercolour.

with a high horizon line. But sometimes the sky is as important, or more so, than the land, so you will need to give a fuller account of it.

Summer trees
The full foliage and dappled sunlight on the trees and undergrowth camouflage the basic shape of the tree trunks and branches.

You may like to practise the three basic cloud formations, which are as follows: white fluffy cumulus clouds in a blue sky; cirrus clouds, sometimes known as 'mare's tails'; and storm clouds, which may have patches of blue showing through. The first two are easy, as they can be achieved by laying a blue wash and then lifting out some of the colour with a piece of cotton or tissue. Storm clouds are best painted wet-in-wet, dropping darker colours into light ones with a well-loaded brush, and again, lifting out highlights while the paint is still wet.

Winter trees and sky *The bare branches and flat light of a winter's day make a starker image.*

Overcast grey rainy skies are not often used in paintings, as they are dull and cast no light on the landscape, but practise clear blue skies, as they are not quite as easy as they look. The sky becomes lighter at the bottom, so you will need to lay a graded wash, starting with a deep blue and gradually fading as you work down the paper by adding progressively more water. For any of these skies, mix up the colours beforehand because if you have to stop to mix up more colour the paint will begin to dry before you want it to, which may result in stripes and blotches.

The perspective of skies

Everything we see is governed by the laws of perspective, and skies are no exception. A common mistake is to make all clouds roughly the same size, but they are much larger directly overhead, because they are nearer to you. Think of the sky as a flattened-out dome, with the rim resting far away on the horizon. There the clouds will appear small and bunched together, with minimal contrasts of tone and colour, while those above you may have clearly defined tones and colours.

Cloud types
A cumulus cloud (left) and a cirrus cloud (right) are completely different in structure. Rainclouds add tremendous atmosphere and are best painted wet-in-wet.

EXERCISE 12

Palm trees by Roger Hutchins

Travel to new places presents us with a variety of potential subjects that may be quite overwhelming. But however exciting the subject may appear, never lose sight of the purely pictorial values, as an

awareness of these will help to simplify decisions about what to draw and what viewpoint to choose. Look for shapes and patterns in the landscape that provide naturally interesting compositions. In this

> **Practice points**
> - IDENTIFYING HIDDEN SHAPES AND PATTERNS
> - BOLD MARK-MAKING WITH CONTÉ CRAYON
> - SUGGESTING MOVEMENT
> - BALANCING TONE AND LINE

example, the angled palm trees form a number of intersecting triangles that give stability to the composition, balanced by the dynamic sweeping diagonals of the fronds, which impart movement and drama to the picture. Conté crayon is an excellent medium for this kind of sketch, as you can use it on its side to rapidly establish blocks of tone and make a wide variety of marks with a sharp corner of the point.

The two main trees form an almost symmetrical triangle, so if you extend the lines to complete the triangle you will find it easier to judge their angles.

STAGE 1
THE FRAMEWORK

■ This central triangle is the key to the composition. It takes a little practice to be able to spot these hidden shapes, but once you have learned to do this you will find the drawing much easier. Work in conté crayon from the outset rather than starting in pencil, as graphite and conté don't mix. You can erase the guidelines later using a putty eraser.

sketching in a light vertical line will also help you to get the angles of the trees right, as you can compare the left and right sides.

The vertical line also cuts across the eye-level line at the point where the trees on the edge of the sand are farthest away. The low horizon emphasises the height of trees and the intensity of the tropical sky.

STAGE 2

PLOT OUT THE TREES

■ Gradually build up the outlines of the trees. The palm trunks will appear more natural if you don't draw perfectly straight lines, and it is easier to create the sweeping curves by drawing them in long strokes, working from the elbow rather than just bending your wrist. The marks you make in this way will be stronger and more confident, and you will also be less likely to smudge the crayon with your hand. It may help to turn your paper so that you can draw the more pronounced curves from the inside of the bend.

Once you have sketched in the main trees you can use them to check the proportions and angles of other elements in the picture. The angle of the frond sweeping in from the left side can be verified by imagining where the line of the midrib would touch the trunk of the big tree and by comparing it to the ones around it. The more features you draw in, the more reference points you'll have available.

The light-coloured frond in the foreground just touches the trunk of one of the most distant palms. Move the entire plant to the right so that it just overlaps the right-hand tree. This gives a greater feeling of depth, and will help the sweep of the foreground frond to lead the eye into the picture.

STAGE 3
ADD TONE

■ Suggest the tone for the sky by using the side of the crayon; then rub over it with your finger to blend and soften it. Don't blend every area of tone, as the contrast between soft and rough marks will add interest and suggest texture. The strokes representing the shadows on the sand should remain unblended, as the white specks left where the crayon does not cover the tooth of the paper help to give a natural sparkle to the sand.

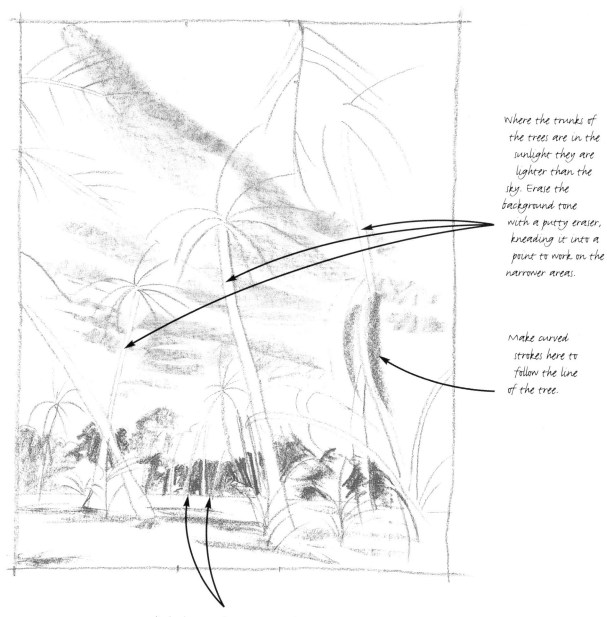

Where the trunks of the trees are in the sunlight they are lighter than the sky. Erase the background tone with a putty eraser, kneading it into a point to work on the narrower areas.

Make curved strokes here to follow the line of the tree.

Establish the deep shadows under the distant trees by blocking in the tone between the white trunks of the trees with the side of the crayon. Make short, heavy strokes at different angles so that small areas of lighter tone are left to suggest form and texture.

STAGE 4
BUILD UP THE TREES

■ To indicate the form and texture of the tree trunks, use a method known as bracelet shading, which involves making short, curving strokes following the cylindrical shapes. Towards the bottoms of the trees, as they begin to come close to the eye-level line, flatten the curves, as the round 'slices' of the tree are seen more edge-on. This hint of perspective will make the trees appear more three-dimensional.

some of the dark leaves on the far sides of the palm-tree tops can be used to frame the outline of the trunks. The trees will seem less like flat cut-outs if you take the far sides of their trunks into account.

Leave the areas of brightest highlight white, along with the area where the light frond crosses the trunk.

The bracelet shading gives a good impression of texture.

start to sketch in the palm fronds, keeping the trees in the background simple, and don't try to draw every blade.

STAGE 5
MAKE DESCRIPTIVE MARKS

■ Draw the midribs of the fronds using a corner of the tip, with the stick held between your thumb and first two fingers, roughly parallel to your knuckles. Pull it in a curving movement in the direction of growth, away from the trunk. Add single blades to the palm fronds by holding the crayon so that one edge of the square end (or a sharp edge of the worn-down tip) touches the paper and move it in a rapid, slightly curving stroke from the base of the blade to the tip, reducing the pressure as you go. Keep rotating the stick so that the angle touching the paper is still acute, which helps to ensure that the stroke will taper to a point. This is easier to do than it is to describe, but it might be wise to practise a few strokes beforehand on a piece of scrap paper. Try not to apply too much pressure, but don't worry if a stick snaps. Short pieces are not wasted, as they can be used on their sides to block in areas of flat tone.

The general direction of most of the lines gives a feeling of life and dynamism to the wind-blown trees.

Draw each blade with a loose, curving stroke in the direction of growth – away from the trunk and midrib.

Some fronds will have visible blades on both sides of the midrib, while on others they will both hang down below the rib. Any irregularity in your strokes will make the leaves look more natural and suggest the way that they move in the wind.

STAGE 6
WORK THE FOREGROUND

■ The darkest marks and greatest contrasts are reserved for the fronds at the top and bottom right, at the front of the picture plane, as these help to frame the view and add a foreground layer to the composition. These need to be handled carefully, which is why they are left until last, other than a few lines to indicate their position. Conté crayon is soft enough to smudge, so when you have completed your drawing spray it with fixative, or you can cover it with tissue or tracing paper if you are storing it in a drawer. If you are working in a sketchbook it may help to begin at the back and work forwards, as the pages are less likely to rub over each other and smudge.

These leaves imply trees above and behind the viewer, and it is important not to treat them as a solid tone. Leave wide enough gaps between the fronds to allow the background to show through.

Don't make the foreground frond that was moved to the right too dark, as the emphasis should be on the flowing curve of its central rib, which leads the eye into the picture. If it were made too dark or solid, it could constitute a visual barrier, disrupting the composition.

Drawing the individual blade-like leaves outwards from the supporting rib will help you to keep the central portion white, as you can control the position of the crayon much better at the static start of a stroke than when it is moving at the end.

EXERCISE 13

Trees in a cornfield
by Janet Whittle

This is a very simple view, and the trees in full leaf make an inviting subject. But as a composition it lacks structure and drama, so the artist has decided to improve on nature to give the drawing more impact. She has increased the angle of the diagonal on the left to lead the eye in towards the trees and made the cast shadows a much more positive feature. She has also pushed the trees back in space so that much of the sky area is cut out. Always consider how you can move features of the landscape around or exaggerate some foreground feature to add interest.

Practice points
- SIMPLIFYING FOLIAGE
- MAKING AN EXCITING COMPOSITION
- CREATING FOREGROUND INTEREST

STAGE I
LOOK FOR THE MAIN SHAPES

■ Always look for the main shapes of the trees first. You may find that it helps to squint your eyes to cut out some of the detail.

Draw the trees just as outlines, but take care with the proportions, looking for important clues such as where the small tree shape intersects the larger one.

The cast shadows make opposing, shallower diagonals that create a lively foreground pattern. In the photograph, the shadows are more or less horizontal.

The eye tends to follow diagonals, so lead the viewer into the picture from the foreground to the focal point.

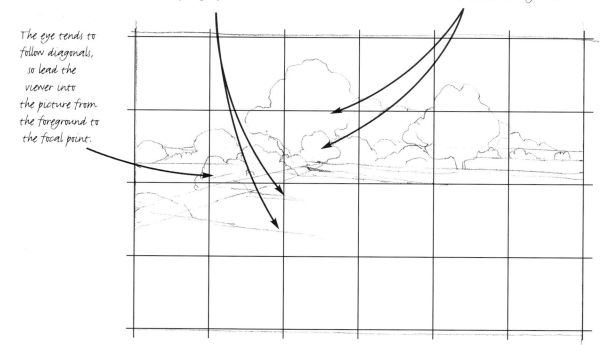

STAGE 2
ADD TONE

■ From the outset, think about what you might simplify and how. You will always see much more detail in a landscape than you need to include. You can often generalise the skies, as an over-detailed treatment of clouds may detract from the main centre of interest, which in this case is the trees.

shade in the distant clumps of trees using an HB pencil, again slanting the strokes. Vary the length of strokes for the trees on the left to give a light suggestion of foliage.

shade in the sky with long strokes, slanting them to add more movement to the composition. Keep it simple to contrast with the complicated tree line.

Using an HB pencil, shade in the shadowed sides of the small bushes and the dark areas of the left-hand tree.

STAGE 3
BUILD UP THE FORMS

■ Large trees like these are made up from many separate and solid-looking clumps of foliage – a series of small shapes that combine to form the main one. Try to identify the clumps and watch how they are defined by the play of light, but don't lose sight of the main shapes.

Pull out the shadows across the field with small diagonal strokes that suggest the grass. Make the strokes smaller towards the distance.

simplify the bushes behind to throw the sunstruck edges of the trees forwards.

Add shading to the right-hand tree, leaving the trunk as white paper. Note that the light is coming from the left, so the darks will be mainly concentrated on the right side.

STAGE 4
STRENGTHEN THE TONES

■ Before starting work on the foreground, you need to build up the tonal contrasts on the trees. It is often easier to decide how to treat the foreground when the main elements of the composition are established. Also, working from top to bottom helps to avoid smudging the drawing with your hand.

Use a 3B pencil to add form and texture to the large trees, making short stabbing strokes at the top, especially on the left-hand tree.

Bearing the direction of the light in mind, shade the dark sides of the background bushes.

Emphasise the deep shadows at the base of the trees with a 9B pencil.

Add a middle tone to the small bushes, leaving the tops as white paper.

STAGE 5
THE FOREGROUND

■ Now you can begin to consider how much detail and tonal contrast the foreground will need. To give a lively feel to the composition, continue the theme of diagonals and curves, with plough lines crossing over the lines of the shadows and tractor marks crossing over these in turn.

Use diagonal strokes to shade in this field, thus ensuring that the eye is taken in towards the trees.

With a 3B pencil, put in dark tones on these trees, following the contours of the bank, and carry them out into the stubble field.

These curving lines echo the curves at the top of the central dark trees, helping to unify the composition.

Lightly draw in the rows of stubble, starting at the back and widening the lines towards the foreground. Draw the tractor lines with small near-vertical strokes, fading out gradually at the centre of the field.

Deepen and widen the tractor marks in the lines of the stubble, and hatch in a tone in the foreground, using first an HB pencil and then a 3B. Make even strokes, feathering towards the field.

Reduce the tonal contrast slightly in the centre of the tree by hatching in a mid-tone with an HB pencil. The tree was previously a little 'jumpy', with too much light/dark contrast in this area.

Add some mid-tone areas of shadow with an HB pencil.

J. WHITTLE

STAGE 6
FINAL ADJUSTMENTS

■ When you have reached this stage in a drawing, stand back from it, propping it up about 1 metre (3 feet) away, and decide whether adjustments need to be made. Here the artist adds a mid-tone to the immediate foreground and the shadows on the left to enhance the sunlit effect.

EXERCISE I4

Trees and gate by Joe Francis Dowden

Drawing trees in winter or early spring teaches you to observe their different skeleton shapes. This is good practice for painting a tree in full leaf, as you will understand its underlying structure. Without their leafy cladding, trees offer certain challenges to the artist. Study the branches carefully, noting their thickness, how they grow from the trunk and the ways in which they can twist downwards or back on themselves. To prevent this very symmetrical composition from becoming too static, the viewpoint incorporates elements at different angles, such as the gate and the slope of the foreground. These lead the viewer towards the centre and give movement to the piece.

Practice points
- OBSERVING A SKELETON TREE SHAPE
- COMPOSITION AROUND A CENTRAL FOCAL POINT
- USING COLOURED PENCILS

STAGE I
THE BASIC SHAPES

■ Use a grid to position the larger elements and angles of the drawing. Sketch the outline of the main branches and the gate, paying attention to the negative shapes and consistency in the thickness of each item.

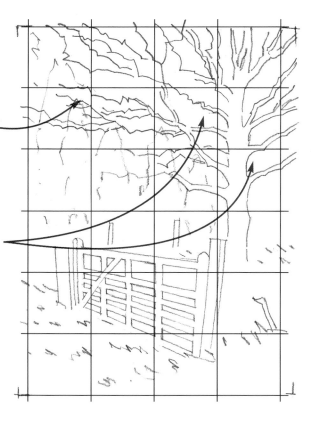

Take special care drawing the branches. One common mistake is to draw them so that they become thicker the farther they are from the trunk.

As you draw, observe the negative spaces between the branches – these will help to confirm that you are creating the correct shapes.

Keep checking the position of the main elements against the grid. If anything does not work within the composition, it is easy at this stage to rub it out and adjust as necessary.

STAGE 2
INITIAL COLOUR

■ You are now ready to start the colour work. Your first step is to add diagonal strokes of lemon yellow which will give a sunlit effect to the drawing. Add further strokes of crimson to the trees and cobalt blue and black over the woodland grass.

The sky and gate will require pure colours later so leave them white.

Build up the black outlines of the branches.

Pencil some of the spaces between the bars in the gate with burnt sienna to echo the warm woodland tones.

The shading in your drawing should be a series of diagonal marks. Try to keep your pencil at an angle between horizontal and vertical throughout and not one of the two. This unifies the drawing and creates a sense of lively movement.

The lemon yellow strokes will add warmth, life, and variation to any colour subsequently pencilled over it.

Start to add colour to the gate. Use lemon yellow for the main gate and define the shadows with black.

To create the combinations of rust, yellow-green, and blue-green in the grass, pencil burnt sienna loosely over the yellow of the grass. Follow with cobalt blue in the background to create a loose weave of pencil lines. Leave plenty of white.

STAGE 3
BUILD UP AND BLEND COLOURS

Working with coloured pencil allows you to incorporate great subtlety of colour in a piece by building up semi-transparent layers of different colours. Having now established most of the colour, you can give the drawing depth by strengthening the darker areas. Make sure you do not press too hard with the pencil or block in areas too solidly, as you risk saturating the paper surface so that it will not be able to accept any further blends of colour.

Strengthen the main tree with short, loose diagonal strokes of burnt sienna and black. Leave a few glimpses of yellow between the pencil lines to give sparkle to the tree. Add crimson and emerald green to the fir trees in the background.

To ensure a strong outline to the gate, pencil the background woodland tones on either side of it up against a piece of card. The card acts as a stencil or mask for the gate.

Allow vibrant flashes of white paper to show through here and there.

Build up woodland tones using loose hatches of burnt sienna, cobalt blue, and emerald green over the underlying lemon yellow. Note how you create new colours where the lines cross each other or go over the white paper.

Carefully build up the gaps in the gate with burnt sienna and emerald green. Add black to the gate and accentuate the shadows on the grass.

The consciously directional hatching and marking of the different colours help to create movement and to encourage the eye to move around the scene.

STAGE 4
ADD DETAIL AND FINAL BLENDS

Bring in final detail and realism by adding a web of smaller boughs and twigs to the existing branches of the tree. Vary the direction in which the branches grow – the smaller ones could grow backward, arch, or crisscross and overlap. These branches need to stand out from the background, so use a dark colour such as black or indigo with a reasonable amount of pressure, and keep the point of your pencil freshly sharpened. For the softer effects of the trees in the distance, you can use less pressure and a more worn-down pencil. This will give lighter tones that blend into the undergrowth.

Incorporate areas of shadow into the foreground by hatching black back and forth with a rounded and softened pencil.

Add the final details of the branches in black.

The contrast of the dark shadow and the white highlight on the gate make this the initial focal point of the sketch. The eye is then led upwards from the right side of the gate to the tree.

FOCUS ON LANDSCAPES

Shadows and reflections

Shadows and reflections can play a major part both in the composition of a landscape sketch and in the colour scheme if you are painting. Reflections, of course, will only be seen if there is an area of water in the subject, but this need not be as large as a lake; small reflections in puddles can be used very effectively to add interest and atmosphere. Shadows also help to explain the lay of the land, so make sure they follow the contours rather than flatten them out.

Shadows

If you want to work up the sketch into a finished painting, take a reference photograph as well. Shadow colours will also alter according to the time of day, so either paint them in at an early stage or make notes about the colours so that you can make them consistent. You don't want to have some parts of the painting with morning shadows and others with afternoon shadows.

The colours of shadows are influenced both by the colour of the ground on which they are cast and by the light source. Shadows on snow, for example, are often quite a strong blue, because the white surface reflects the sky. Those on grass will reflect the sky to a lesser extent so that you will see both blues and greens, with the overall colour usually cooler than in the sunlit areas. Shadow colours can be exaggerated to give extra punch to the painting: you can bring in more blues and mauves, add a touch of warm colour to a cool shadow, and vice versa.

Shadows on grass
The sunlight that falls on this tree from the right casts a long grey-tinted shadow across the grass.

Shadows on snow
The artist has exaggerated the colours in this scene, using mauve to warm up the blue shadows and reflections on the water.

Mirror image

Horizontal marks indicate surface of water.

Reflections

A still surface of water viewed from a distance produces an exact mirror image of the landscape features above, but if you copy this effect too faithfully you will lose the horizontal surface of the water. Mute the colours or blur the lines slightly, and consider introducing one or two ripples, or perhaps some floating leaves, to suggest the water surface. When a reflection is closer to you, you will also see some of the colours of the mud or sand beneath the water, so if you are painting the reflection of a boat or rock, incorporate this colour into the reflection.

Mirror image

Scattered reflections

Drawing the water surface
The reflective surfaces of moving water sparkle and scatter reflections in an unpredictable way, whereas still water allows for a strong, unbroken reflection.

When the water surface is broken into ripples or wavelets, there will be many small reflective surfaces lying at different angles, so the reflections will be scattered in unpredictable ways, both sideways and downwards. These broken reflections create very exciting effects, but they do require careful observation and a degree of simplification. If you are working on the spot, try to give an impression rather than a literal account, using broken marks or brushstrokes and varying the edges from soft to hard. If you are working from a photo, beware of trying to recreate every ripple and every nuance of light and shade. Too much fussy detail will sacrifice the sense of movement that is all-important in such a subject.

Mirror image Use a little artistic license to blur the surface of very still water, even if the surface is a mirror image in reality.

EXERCISE **15**

Sunset over water
by Michael Lawes

There can be few people who are not excited by the glowing colours of sunsets and the way they can transform an ordinary landscape into something new and magical. But sunsets do present a challenge to the artist, not only because the effects seldom last long enough to sketch on the spot, but also because it is all too easy to sentimentalise them and produce a rather clichéd painting.

Practice points
- **MAKING EXPRESSIVE PASTEL MARKS**
- **CREATING SURFACE TEXTURE**
- **UNIFYING THE COLOURS**

The artist has avoided the latter pitfall by using energetic and expressive pastel marks rather than blending the colours by rubbing them into one another, giving the sketch a lively sense of immediacy and movement. He has also worked on watercolor paper, which has sufficient texture to break up the strokes, leaving little specks of white that make the colours sparkle.

STAGE 1
THE FRAMEWORK

■ Start with a pencil drawing, keeping the lines as light as possible, as graphite is slightly greasy and tends to repel the pastel colour laid on top. Then block in the deep greens of the land using two shades of olive green. These dark areas will give the drawing some solidity.

Make diagonal hatching strokes, but vary them slightly so that some are more upright than others.

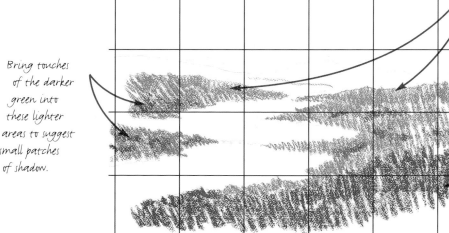

Bring touches of the darker green into these lighter areas to suggest small patches of shadow.

It is important not to overfill the grain of the paper in the early stages, or it will be difficult to lay more colours on top, so keep the strokes open and relatively light.

STAGE 2

ESTABLISH THE BRIGHT COLOURS

■ The dark greens provide a key that helps you to decide on the colours needed for the sky and distant hills. If you started with the reds and yellows, which is bound to be a temptation, you would probably get them wrong, as you would be judging them against nothing but white paper. It is vital to see colours and tones in relation to one another.

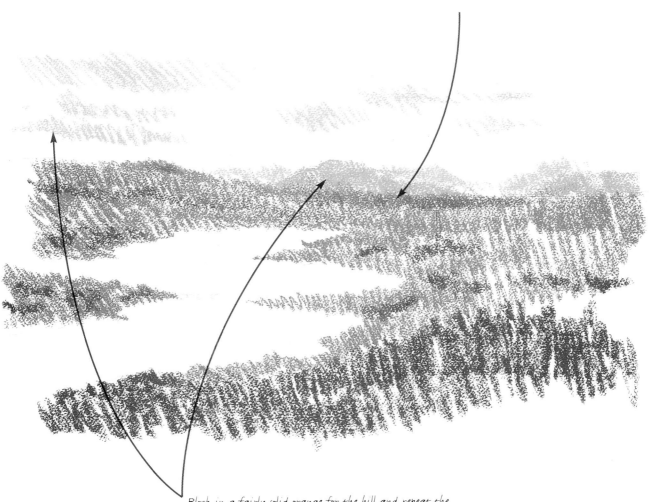

Don't be afraid to use a really strong red here, as you will be modifying the colours as you work. Bring a little of the red down into the green to tie the two areas together.

Block in a fairly solid orange for the hill and repeat the same colour in the sky, using lighter, more open strokes.

STAGE 3
PAINT THE SKY AND LAKE

■ Now that you have the basic structure in place, with the tones and colours established, you can paint the sky and lake, using lemon yellow with touches of orange, and leaving the paper white for the sun and its reflection. But don't work on just one area in isolation; as you go on, try to assess the painting as a whole, adding more colour and tone to the foreground areas to balance the vivid colours.

Take some of the light yellow used for the sky down over the hills so that they blend together slightly. Blending by overlaying colours produces a more exciting effect than rubbing them into one another, which can result in bland or muddy passages of colour.

Make a light suggestion of clouds with short strokes of orange and bring in orange at the top of the sky, varying the strokes so that some are farther apart than others.

Describe the flat surface of the lake with horizontal strokes, using two shades of yellow. On the left side, keep the strokes more open, as you will be laying more colour in this area.

Darken the foreground with indigo to provide a deep tone and a touch of complementary contrast – indigo is a purplish colour, and yellow is the complementary of the mauves and purples.

The overlaid strokes of colour mix optically, producing a much livelier effect than can be achieved with solid colour.

The strokes of the orange sky colour among the greens help to tie these two areas together, easing the transition from middleground to background.

Make strong horizontal strokes of orange here to echo the clouds at the top of the sky.

To push the distant hills back in space, build up the strength of tone with more indigo, laid on fairly heavily.

STAGE 4
TIE THE ELEMENTS TOGETHER

■ Darken the tone in the foreground so that it comes forwards to create a greater sense of space. The best way to unify the composition is to make color 'echoes' by bringing in touches of the sky colour into the land.

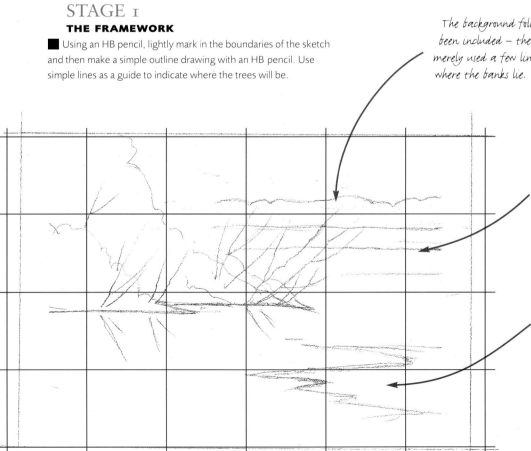

Reflections in still water
by Janet Whittle

A tranquil scene like this invites a delicate watercolour treatment, with soft blends and a harmonious colour scheme consisting mainly of blues, yellows and greens – hues that are close together on the colour wheel. The artist has played down the patches of bright red that can be seen in the photograph, as these would introduce a jarring note, and has merely suggested the flowers, keeping the colours relatively muted.

Practice points
- **WORKING WET-IN-WET**
- **MASKING HIGHLIGHTS**
- **CONTRASTING HARD AND SOFT EDGES**

STAGE 1
THE FRAMEWORK

■ Using an HB pencil, lightly mark in the boundaries of the sketch and then make a simple outline drawing with an HB pencil. Use simple lines as a guide to indicate where the trees will be.

The background foliage has not been included – the artist merely used a few lines to show where the banks lie.

Draw the line of the far bank in first, moving it up the page to allow a slightly wider gap between it and the trees on the left.

Artistic licence has been used here. The artist altered the right-hand reeds as a balance and brought them further into the sketch to lead the eye in.

STAGE 2
DRAW AND BLOCK IN

■ Working on watercolour paper, make an outline drawing with pencil to place the main features and then mix up the first washes so that you don't run out when in the middle of a wash. The colours you will be using for the first stage are as follows: cobalt blue; cadmium yellow; a mixture of cadmium yellow and viridian; and a mixture of viridian and burnt umber.

Load the large brush with cobalt blue and paint a wash over the background trees, changing to cadmium yellow halfway down to the shoreline.

Reload the brush with more cadmium yellow and lay a wash over the trees on the left. Then, while the paper is still damp, dip the brush into the mid-green mixture (cadmium yellow and viridian) and drop in some of this darker colour, taking care not to cover too much of the yellow.

You will be working wet-in-wet, so dampen the paper down to the shoreline with a large brush and clean water. Take the wet brush over the paper twice, as it needs to be evenly damp.

Now use the darkest color (the viridian and burnt umber mixture), running a broken line along the edge of the lake. The paint will dry with a hard edge where it meets dry paper and a soft one above, where it runs into the other colours.

STAGE 3
BUILD UP THE BACKGROUND

■ You will need masking fluid for this stage, and again, mix up the washes before you start – this is a good habit to get into for watercolour work. You will require a mixture of cobalt blue and indigo, indigo on its own, and rose madder.

Mask out the tops of the smaller trees on the left-hand bank, making small brushmarks to describe the leaf texture, and leave to dry. Wash the brush immediately, as masking fluid cannot be removed once it has dried.

Dampen the background again, going over the masking, then use the tip of the brush to drop in small strokes of the cobalt blue and indigo mixture. As you work forwards to the hedge, use darker indigo and define the shore with the same colour. Drop in a few patches of rose madder while the paper is still damp, then leave to dry.

STAGE 4
PAINT THE TREES

■ You will be painting the darker tones on the left-hand trees with the same colours used for the previous step – the varied blues laid over the original yellow will mix on the paper to produce a range of greens. Remove the masking fluid, either with an eraser or by rubbing gently with a finger, and then paint the foliage, darkening the tones towards the water.

Because the fluid was laid over the first yellow wash with darker colours laid on top, the leaves stand out as pale yellow shapes. Masking fluid is very useful for small highlights with complicated edges.

To give a hint of the red flowers among the foliage, paint over the yellow with diluted cobalt blue, then drop in a little rose madder while the paint is still damp.

Let the first wash dry before lightly touching in the flowers. The red is muted by the greens and yellows below so that it does not stand out too strongly.

Paint the tree and branches running through the foliage with a rigger brush and a mixture of indigo and rose madder.

Paint the whole of the water with horizontal strokes, starting with cobalt blue and darkening with a cobalt blue and indigo mixture as you come forwards.

STAGE 5
PAINT THE LAKE

■ You will be working wet-in-wet again for this stage, so when the foliage is completely dry, dampen the paper again in the area of the lake, leaving a little strip of dry paper beneath the left-hand foliage and a larger strip at the far bank. The colours are the same as those used for the two stages of the trees, plus viridian on its own, so mix up some more if needed.

While this wash is still damp, paint in the reflections of the trees. Use a clean, slightly damp brush to lift out a couple of horizontal ripples to break up the reflection and add a blush of green on the right for the reeds.

To create a strong passage of colour in the foreground, bring in the rose madder used for the flowers and paint strokes of fairly strong viridian on either side.

STAGE 6
COMPLETE THE SKETCH
■ The only feature that still remains to be painted is the grassy area on the right, which balances the trees and completes the composition. When you have painted this, prop the sketch up a short distance away from you so that you can view it as a whole and decide whether any final adjustments are needed.

Let the washes dry and then use the dark green again to paint in some individual grasses with the tip of the brush. Paint a few over the water too, using a mid-tone green.

To make the trees show up more strongly, deepen behind them with a mixture of cobalt blue and a touch of indigo, then brighten them with a touch of yellow.

Using a light- and a dark-green tone (mixtures of the colours used for the trees), paint the grass, and while still damp, put in a strong dark at the bottom. This will produce a hard edge where the paint meets the dry paper, and a soft one above.

Dampen the water area beneath the grasses and drop in the reflection, using the same colours.

Scrape out a few highlights in the water with a knife to accentuate the horizontal surface.

Media Technique Directory

Dry media such as wooden and carbon pencils, charcoal, soft and hard pastels, carrés and colour pencils are flexible tools for sketchers. Although the choice is seemingly endless, your art supplier will be able to advise you. Wherever possible, buy pencils and pastels singly, rather than in boxed sets.

▲ Create areas of tone using a soft pencil. The heavier the pressure, the darker the tone.

WOODEN PENCIL

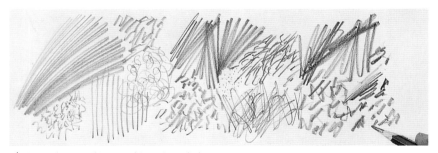

▲ A wooden pencil is a graphite strip sealed into a wooden case. It can be used on a variety of different surfaces to produce a wide range of linear effects. Note the difference between the lines made with a hard B, a 2B and a soft 6B pencil (left to right).

▲ Lines can be hatched or cross-hatched with a wooden pencil to build up areas of varying tone and density. Here the top of the cliff is cross-hatched, while the shadows down the sides are hatched.

▲ Tone can be varied and lightened by blending different weights of pencil with a finger, torchon, or soft eraser.

CARBON PENCIL

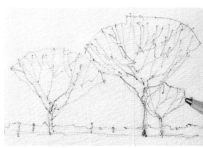

▲ A carbon pencil is compressed charcoal sealed into a wooden case. It is a soft pencil that gives a rich black line with very little pressure. Used on damp paper, it gives an even denser, velvety black line.

Cartridge paper and pads

Cartridge paper is available in a range of weights and comes in sheets, rolls, pads and sketchbooks. Its primary use is for drawing with dry media and ink, and it is not ideal for pastel, charcoal or watercolour.

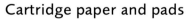

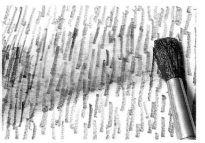

▲ A line made by a carbon pencil will spread and soften when washed over, making some wonderful greys.

CHARCOAL

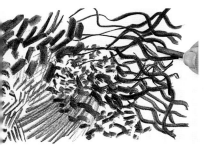

▲ Thin stick charcoal produces expressive, linear strokes, and thick marks can be made by using the charcoal on its side. You can vary the thickness of the stroke by changing the angle of the charcoal stick on the page.

▲ Create highlights in an area of tone – or correct mistakes – by lifting out the charcoal with a putty eraser (knead the eraser into a point for small details). This can produce a variety of effects, from sharp lines to texture and highlights.

▼ Thin charcoal is a useful medium to use for building up a web of hatched or crosshatched lines or marks.

▼ You can build up large mid-tone areas by using a charcoal stick on its side and then smudging with a finger, rag, blending stump, or brush.

SOFT PASTEL

Pastel sheets and pads
Most pastel artists will use specially textured pastel papers that will hold several layers of dry pastel dust without becoming saturated. Pastel papers are available in a wide range of colours.

▲ Areas of colour can be built up quickly by blending with a dry brush. Pastels mix particularly well with other drawing media, including coloured pencil, watercolour, and gouache.

◀ Soft pastels are the most commonly used pastels and offer the largest choice of tints and tones. Crossing one set of hatched lines with another increases the density of colour and tone.

▲ Used on its side, pastel makes a broad area of solid colour. Take care to protect your work, as soft pastels do crumble easily and can be messy to use.

▲ The finger is an ideal tool for blending and can be used to vary the tone density, as demonstrated here for aerial perspective.

HARD PASTEL

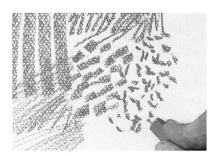

▲ Hard pastels are usually square, but can be sharpened to a point with a sharp craft knife. Use the end or sharp edge of the pastel to create lines, strokes, dashes and dots.

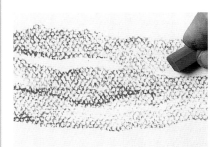

▲ Using a pastel on its edge, but changing the angle as you work, can give a line of varying width, which is useful when sketching moving water.

▼ The powdery quality of pastel makes it possible to blend two or more colours together. Here the texture of the leaves is created by rubbing the pastel.

▲ To soften and blur edges or modify, blend with a finger, brush, rag or torchon.

PASTEL PENCIL

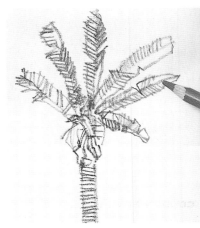

▲ Pastel pencils are made of a strip of hard pastel secured inside a wooden case. They are ideal for line work, especially when working detail into a sketch made with soft or hard pencils. Sharpen pastel pencils with a traditional pencil sharpener or craft knife.

▲ Smudge the line with your finger or a torchon to soften your sketch and blend the colours.

Using fixative

Fixative leaves a matte layer of resin that coats and holds any loose pigment dust in place. It is usually used with charcoal and pastel sketches. Fixative is available in aerosol cans, and in bottles that use a pump action or need a diffuser, and should always be sprayed away from the face and clothing.

▲ Used on its edge, a conté stick will make a variety of different textural marks; however, a carré pencil will make a finer line.

COLOUR PENCIL

▼ Build up density, tone and texture by hatching and cross-hatching lines of colour. From a distance, two colours that are closely hatched will appear as a solid blend of the two colours.

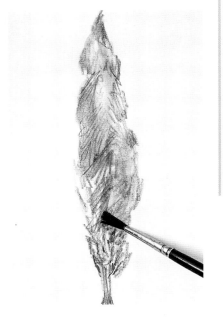

CONTÉ STICKS/CARRÉ PENCILS

▲ Use a conté stick on its side to produce a block of solid colour.

▲ An eraser can be used to make corrections, as well as to produce specific tonal or textural effects. Here it has been used to lift out highlights.

◄ Washing water over coloured pencil marks – wet-on-dry – will add more depth to your sketch.

OIL PASTELS

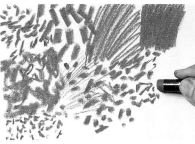

▲ Oil pastels can be opaque, semi-transparent or transparent. They can be used to make fine linear strokes and textural marks.

▲ The consistency of oil pastels is perfect for making effects with sgraffito, or scratching techniques. Here, a craft knife has been used to scratch out blades of grass.

BALLPOINT PEN

▼ Although ballpoint pens produce lines of uniform width, the end result can look lively and spontaneous.

Acetate and tracing paper

Tracing paper is used to transfer drawings from one surface to another, while acetate is often used to make up grids (see page 11).

TECHNICAL PEN

▲ A technical pen delivers ink to the paper through a narrow metal tube, producing an unvarying line width that is unaffected by hand pressure. It is ideal for detailed linework such as drawing leaves.

MARKER AND FELT-TIP PENS

▼ Use a wide-tipped marker pen to create blocks of colour.

▼ A wide range of marker and felt-tip pens is available that can produce a variety of lines and marks. Here, a fine-tipped pen has been used to hatch and make marks.

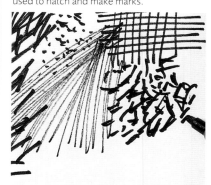

▲ You can mix colours by laying one colour over another, usually working light to dark.

▲ Markers are either water- or solvent-based. You can make interesting effects by working into drawings with water.

INK

▼ Vary the angle of the brush or the pressure on the paper to alter the thickness of the line.

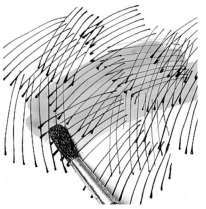

▲ If water-resistant ink is used, as here, you can apply tonal washes to linework. If the ink is water-soluble, you may need to redraw essential marks when the wash is dry.

▲ Perfect for clear blue skies, a graded wash is a variation on the flat wash. However, each time you make a horizontal stroke, add more water to the mix, making it slightly lighter (or add more paint to make it darker).

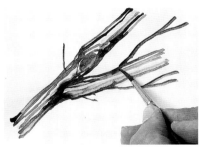

▲ To create tone with a brush, dilute the ink with water.

WATERCOLOUR

▲ Before you begin, make sure that you have mixed enough paint to complete the task. A flat wash needs to be applied at a slight 20-degree angle. Load a large wash brush with paint and, starting at the top, make a steady horizontal stroke across the paper. The next stroke will need to overlap the first slightly.

Watercolour pads

Watercolour paper can be bought in separate sheets or in pads or sketchbooks of varying sizes.

▼ A dip pen is flexible and results in expressive lines of varying widths, depending on the pressure you put on the nib. Its ability to use a wide range of nibs makes it a versatile tool. Used here over a dry wash, the dip pen and ink create crisp spring leaves.

Watercolour paper

Watercolour paper is woven, acid-free and usually white. It comes in degrees of thickness and in three different textures: rough, cold-pressed (also known as NOT) and hot-pressed. Machine-made watercolour paper is the most inexpensive of watercolour papers, but may distort when wet. Mould-made papers are more durable and less resistant to distortion. The best, but most expensive, type is handmade.

▲ This wash is similar to the graded wash, but you need to change colour part of the way through the process with a clean brush. This effect is perfect for sunsets.

▲ Apply wet paint over or into an area that is already wet with paint. Depending on how wet the base layer is, the technique results in colours flowing and blending together.

▲ Lift out areas of wet paint with a tissue. This can be used as an erasing technique, and also for special effects such as fluffy clouds.

▲ Remove excess paint from the brush, and then drag it over the paper surface. Stiffer bristle brushes are best for this technique.

▲ A rigger brush is a fine, long brush that is ideal for painting branches of trees and twigs.

▲ Brush masking fluid onto the paper on the areas you wish to preserve. Masking fluid can be applied with a brush, pen or finger.

Stretching paper

Most paper will swell and buckle if it is wet. When working with wet media such as watercolour, stretch the paper in advance to avoid ruining your work.

1 Place your paper on a large board.

▲ Once the masking fluid is dry, it will repel liquid paint, protecting the area beneath.

2 Measure and cut pieces of adhesive paper tape, to fit around the edge of the paper.

3 Dampen the sheet of paper in a tray of clean water.

▲ Once the paint is dry, gently rub off the masking solution with a finger.

▲ Sgraffito, or scratching out, can be done with any sharp implement. Here, the artist scratches out highlights in grass with the tip of a craft knife.

4 Lay the paper on the board. Dampen the strips of paper tape and lay each strip along the edge of the paper, with one-third of the tape covering the paper and the rest covering the board.

5 Smooth the surface of the tape down with the sponge. Gently wipe the excess water from the paper and leave to dry until the paper is taut. When it is dry, remove the paper from the board by cutting away the tape with a craft knife.

Suppliers

Many of the materials used in this book can be purchased at good art shops. Alternatively, the suppliers listed below can direct you to the retailer nearest you.

NORTH AMERICA

Asel Art Supply
2701 Cedar Springs
Dallas, TX 75201
Toll Free 888-ASELART (for outside
    Dallas only)
Tel (214) 871-2425
Fax (214) 871-0007
www.aselart.com

Cheap Joe's Art Stuff
374 Industrial Park Drive
Boone, NC 28607
Toll Free 800-227-2788
Fax 800-257-0874
www.cjas.com

Daler-Rowney USA
4 Corporate Drive
Cranbury, NJ 08512-9584
Tel (609) 655-5252
Fax (609) 655-5852
www.daler-rowney.com

Daniel Smith
P.O. Box 84268
Seattle, WA 98124-5568
Toll Free 800-238-4065
www.danielsmith.com

Dick Blick Art Materials
P.O. Box 1267
Galesburg, IL 61402-1267
Toll Free 800-828-4548
Fax 800-621-8293
www.dickblick.com

Flax Art & Design
240 Valley Drive
Brisbane, CA 94005-1206
Toll Free 800-343-3529
Fax 800-352-9123
www.flaxart.com

Grumbacher Inc.
2711 Washington Blvd.
Bellwood, IL 60104
Toll Free 800-323-0749
Fax (708) 649-3463
www.sanfordcorp.com/grumbacher

Hobby Lobby
More than 90 retail locations throughout
the US. Check the yellow pages or the
website for the location nearest you.
www.hobbylobby.com

New York Central Art Supply
62 Third Avenue
New York, NY 10003
Toll Free 800-950-6111
Fax (212) 475-2513
www.nycentralart.com

Pentel of America, Ltd.
2805 Torrance Street
Torrance, CA 90509
Toll Free 800-231-7856
Tel: (310) 320-3831
Fax (310) 533-0697
www.pentel.com

Winsor & Newton Inc.
PO Box 1396
Piscataway, NY 08855
Toll Free 800-445-4278
Fax (732) 562-0940
www.winsornewton.com

UNITED KINGDOM

Berol Ltd.
Oldmeadow Road
King's Lynn
Norfolk PE30 4JR
Tel 01553 761221
Fax 01553 766534
www.berol.com

Daler-Rowney
P.O. Box 10
Bracknell, Berks R612 8ST
Tel 01344 424621
Fax 01344 860746
www.daler-rowney.com

Pentel Ltd.
Hunts Rise
South Marston Park
Swindon, Wilts SN3 4TW
Tel 01793 823333
Fax 01793 820011
www.pentel.co.uk

The John Jones Art Centre Ltd.
The Art Materials Shop
4 Morris Place
Stroud Green Road
London N4 3JG
Tel 020 7281 5439
Fax 020 7281 5956
www.johnjones.co.uk

Winsor & Newton
Whitefriars Avenue
Wealdstone, Harrow
Middx HA3 5RH
Tel 020 8427 4343
Fax 020 8863 7177
www.winsornewton.com

Index

Credits

Quarto would like to thank and acknowledge the following for permission to reproduce the pictures that appear in this book.

Key: b=bottom, t=top, c=centre, l=left, r=right
Penny Cobb 30t, 64t; **Roger Hutchins** 28c, 56tr, 63t, 77t;
Geoff Kersey 57t, 93b; **Janet Whittle** 3t, 10t, 11t, 19, 29b,
63b, 76tr, 92, 93t; **Jim Woods** 38tr, 57b

Ian Sidaway for demonstrating the media techniques shown on pages 102–109.

All other photographs and illustrations are the copyright of Quarto Publishing plc. While every effort has been made to credit contributors, we would like to apologise in advance if there have been any omissions or errors.